THE SIMPLICITY OF SPIRITUALITY

The Simplicity of Spirituality

An Introduction

EBENEZER AGBOOLA

The Agboola Ministries

Contents

Dedication   vii
Introduction   ix

1	The Realms	1
2	Come Alive	29
3	Stay Alive	45
4	The Growth Process	96
5	Conclusion	120

New Believer's Prayer   123
Contact the Author   125
About the Book   127
Other Books by the Author   129
About the Author   130

The Simplicity of Spirituality
Copyright © 2022 by Ebenezer Agboola

All rights reserved. No part of this book may be reproduced in any manner whatsoever without written permission except in the case of brief quotations embodied in critical articles and reviews.

Scripture quotes marked (KJV) are taken from the King James Version of the Bible.
Scripture quotes marked (NKJV) are taken from the New King James Version, Copyright © 1982 Thomas Nelson. All rights reserved.

Scripture quotations are taken from the Holy Bible, New Living Translation, copyright ©1996, 2004, 2007, 2013, 2015 by Tyndale House Foundation. Used by permission of Tyndale House Publishers, Inc., Carol Stream, Illinois 60188. All rights reserved.

ISBN: 978-1-7775-0297-3 (e)
ISBN: 978-1-7775-0296-6 (sc)

Cover Design by Shimoma Kizito.

All rights reserved. No part of this book may be reproduced in any manner whatsoever without written permission except in the case of brief quotations embodied in critical articles and reviews.

First Printing, 2022

Dedication

To my Father in Heaven. You went to great lengths to show Your love. You made the relationship and growth in You simple. Thank You for Your love.

To my savior and Lord—Jesus. You are the Love of God in the flesh (**John 3:16**). The simplicity of spirituality is only attainable because You died on the cross for humanity. Without You, I will not know or experience the love of my Father in heaven. Thank You for Your sacrifice on the cross.

To my indispensable helper—The Holy Spirit. Thank You for being the seal of my salvation (**Ephesians 1:13**). My exposure and guidance through the light of this book is because of You. You persuaded, helped and encouraged me to obey even when I had no idea. You make complicated things extremely simple. Thank You for being there to lead and guide me always.

To the vessels of honor that God used to assist in bringing this light to fruition, thank you for your tireless and diligent effort.

To my spiritual father, Pastor Emmanuel Adewusi, I am grateful to God for your life. The doors Jesus opened daily through you led to much content in this book. May Jesus continue to replenish you abundantly. Amen.

To my wife, Tumininu Agboola. Thank you for being so understanding. You are a God-given treasure to my life. I love you.

To every child of God, particularly those who have paved the way by the Spirit of God to the simplicity of spirituality, I bless the name of the Lord for you. Thank you.

Introduction

It was a regular evening after spending time with God; the Lord asked me a question. Do you know what has helped you to attain your current spiritual height? I thought about it and realized that I did not know. However, I was confident that it wasn't just one thing; it was a combination of many things. Hence I said, "Lord, I don't know." He responded, "exactly; if it were something tedious, hard or complicated, you would have known. Now, I want you to write a book titled—The Simplicity of Spirituality." From this encounter, the Lord began to guide me through some practices that quickened my spiritual growth. Therefore, this book was written in obedience to God's instruction.

As you can imagine, my immediate thought was, what do I know? But with the help of the Holy Spirit, I began to realize that God has taught me a lot over time. There were steps that I took in the past without fully understanding their implications and effect on my spiritual growth. As the saying goes, there is a reaction for every action—a cause is followed by a consequence.

In the same way, the actions we take in the physical trigger spiritual effects. For example, there was a time I began to experience specific blessings that, to my knowledge, I had never asked God for. As a teacher, by calling, I became curious. So, I went to God in prayer to inquire. I said, Lord, Your word says, "Ask, and it shall be given" (**Matthew 7:7**). You are not a man that You should lie (**Numbers 23:19**). Also, as per scriptures, Your word is Your bond (**Matthew 24:35**). Father, I didn't ask for all these blessings. And the Lord said, son, when you prayed in the Spirit (**Romans 8:26**), you asked for all these blessings. From then on, I understood the mystery and impact of Spirit-led prayers, and I subsequently did most of my prayers in the Spirit. Other than personal declarations, I rarely pray in my understanding. Some concepts in this book were given by revelation from God; these concepts have also helped me in my times of need. Although I had no idea of its impact at the time of implementation, as I sought God and wrote this book, I began to understand its spiritual magnitude.

Another significant incident occurred a few years ago. After some years away from my parents, I decided to visit. My Mom was concerned about my safety because it had been a while since I left home. So, she decided to seek prayers for my travelling mercies. She consulted a Prophet to agree with her in prayer. To my mother's amazement, the woman of God said, do not worry about your son. My Mom asked why? The Prophet responded, "He is fire on his own." Upon my arrival, my Mom narrated the event to my Dad and me. I smiled and said, Mom, I am no fire, but my God is a consuming fire (**Hebrews 12:29**). It is imperative to state that, at this point, I had just started spending more time with God regularly. Some of the things that made me a spiritual fire in God are highlighted in this book by the Spirit of God.

Growing in your walk with God is not a process you have to struggle with; it is pretty simple. God is not complicated, as many people may believe Him to be. Yes, God is unfathomable. However, His immeasurable love has made building a relationship with Him simple. As you read on, you will come across practical tools the Lord gave me, which have been helping me grow spiritually. Don't be a cherry-picker that chooses only what is most desirable. Be intentional as you read, and allow yourself to assimilate as much as possible. Strive to follow the path emphasized in this book consistently, and you will realize excellent results in your spiritual walk with God.

God inspired the details in this book from the life experiences I have had. However, with God, there is always more to know and experience. You can search His depths and still only be scratching the surface. As you progress through this book, I pray that God gives you insight and understanding. May you begin to see how simple it is to grow in God continuously in Jesus' name. Amen.

However, according to **Proverbs 4:18 (NLT)**, *the way of the righteous is like the first gleam of dawn, which shines ever brighter until the full light of day.* This scripture implies that the information here is only a foundation. There is always more and more in God. You will draw closer to God as you walk in the steps provided. The closer you are to God, the more instructions and steps He will give you. Therefore, this is not the holy grail of growth in God but rather a starting point. God bless you.

Chapter 1

The Realms

Two realms are known to us—the physical and the spiritual. The focus of our study in this book is the spiritual realm. However, discussing the spiritual without understanding the physical realm will create confusion. We will briefly delve into both realms to gain a holistic understanding of our topic. It is important to note that since these two realms are connected, they are also mutually exclusive.

The Word of God is the most excellent tool ever given to understand the mysteries of God. It is a reliable source for grasping the truth. In **John 4:24 NLT**, the Bible reveals the truth that *God is Spirit*. Then in **Genesis 1:26 NLT**, we come to realize God's intention for making man, *"Let us make human beings in our image, to be like us."* Man was made to be "*like*" God. Therefore, humans are gods but not God (**Psalm 82:6**). Man is a spirit being like God, but we see a difference when the Bible further explains that God formed man from the dust of the ground. In accordance with **John 3:6 NKJV** (*that which is born of the flesh is flesh*), we can conclude that man was created to be in the likeness of God and not the embodiment of the fullness of God. Hence, there are critical distinctions between the creator and His creation. The body of man, which was made out of the earth's dust by God, gives man the ability to exist on the earth. It is essential to mention that the man here, Adam, contained both the male and the female at this time of creation (**Genesis 1:27**). So, this concept applies to both men and women.

In **Genesis 1:27 NLT**, we saw that God's masterpiece came to life; in one breath, a molded clay sculpture became a living being. Before the breath of God, man was simply a lifeless sculpture in the hands of God. It was the breath of God that connected man's spirit to his body. Hence man exists in both the physical and the spiritual realm (**John 3:6**).

What we just explained is the biology of God's handiwork. From man's external and internal composition, we see how God designed man to be a spirit being with a soul and living in a body. A man's soul is the interface between the spiritual and physical realms. Information is downloaded from a man's spirit and transmitted to his body via his soul and vice versa.

An emphasis is placed on the soul because of the vital role it plays. **Mark 8:36-37 & Romans 12:2** helps us understand that our souls become the main focus area of development after we come to God through Jesus Christ.

Now that we have established how God created man, we can further advance our understanding by digging deeper into the spiritual and physical realms.

Definition

Everything that God does, He does with intention and detail. Through the process of creation, God intentionally created man last. In other words, He saved the best part for last. God created everything in preparation for the unique beings He would give His Spirit and breath. I can imagine God beautifying the garden of Eden while thinking about how astonished Adam and Eve would be when they finally saw the garden. It has been clear from the beginning; God created the physical realm for man! God stepped into the physical to create something beautiful out of seemingly nothing. The God of the universe existed before it all. Before He established the physical realm, He was already there hovering (**Genesis 1:1-3 NLT**).

The first thing we must understand is that God is Spirit. Although He created the physical realm and manifests in it, His primary place of existence is in the spiritual realm. Given this understanding, we can conclude that the spiritual realm existed before the physical realm and is also superior to the physical realm.

Everything that exists in the realm of the spirit is spirit. The spirit of man exists in this realm. To operate in this domain, one must adhere to spiritual principles. Often people become fearful when discussing this topic due to a deficiency in understanding. You will only be able to fathom the depth you can access spiritually if the light of knowledge on how to navigate the spiritual realm is shed. It is, therefore, our advantage to learn how to thrive in the spiritual realm.

When we apply physical principles, we experience physical growth. Likewise, when we apply spiritual principles, we will experience spiritual growth. My aim here is to refrain from writing out rules for first-timers to follow in the spiritual realm. Instead, I intend to establish the basics for you and point you in the right direction for growth.

Many bold new believers ask: If God made all things, as established in **Isaiah 44:24**, who created God? Questions like this make me excited! I love the curiosity that fuels a new believer's heart to know God more. In response to this question, we must understand that the physical realm is limited. Our life is transient (**Psalm 103:15-16**); hence our knowledge will always be limited due to the nature of our life in the physical. In other words, our physicality cannot be trusted with certain eternal spiritual information. There was more before we came to be, and there will be more after we pass on.

In comparison, God exists in the spiritual realm, where there is no limitation. Such a question cannot be answered definitively because there are certain things we cannot know while on earth. Sometimes, God will transport a person from the physical realm to the spiritual realm to give them insight into spiritual matters, which they wouldn't be privy to in the physical realm (**2 Corinthians 12:2-4**). Such an encounter can be a trance, vision, dream, etc. Humans will never understand the full details of God's existence during their existence on earth.

Think about it for a second! God had to hide Moses when He passed by him in **Exodus 33**. Yet, despite God shielding Moses from the total exposure of the weight of His glory, there was still evidence on Moses' face that He encountered God. Moreover, Moses' glistening face was so unbearable that it was difficult for the Israelites to look at him afterwards (**Exodus 34**).

Attempting to understand God's existence is futile. Some information is classified for the afterlife. In heaven, we will exist entirely in the spiritual realm and not be limited by anything (**Matthew 22:30 & Luke 20:36**).

The unlimited nature of the spiritual realm makes it superior to the physical. Therefore, any physical law can be nullified in the spiritual realm because the spiritual realm controls the physical.

Our life is a result of our physical and spiritual composition. It just so happens that this divine composition has no middle ground. We are either very spiritual or very physical (**Romans 8:5**). The result we manifest is based on the side we give more of ourselves (**Galatians 6:8**). For example, suppose you focused on your spiritual growth, and as a result, you experienced spiritual depths; your physicality might give way and lead to an out of body experience, or even physical death (**2 Corinthians 12:2**). I believe this is one of many possible reasons why some children of God might leave the earth sooner than anticipated.

A classic example was illustrated for us in **Genesis 5:23-24**. Enoch lived for 365 years; he also walked in close fellowship with God. Then, one day he disappeared because God took him. This incident gives us insight that our spiritual depth increases as we walk with God. We can say that Enoch maxed out the depth of the spirituality that his physicality could withstand. Hence, God had to take him; he had to die physically. The moment we die in the physical realm, we exist solely in the spiritual realm, where there is no limitation to what we can see and know.

THE PHYSICAL

One of the world's most excellent search engines, Google, provides us with two fascinating definitions. First, the physical is anything relating to the body, excluding the mind. Second, the physical can be identified as what we perceive through our senses—tangible or concrete. It is important to note that the physical has everything to do with the body (**John 3:6**).

Suppose you study the intricacies of engineering designs. In that case, you will realize that products are designed for their specific environment and operating context. For instance, various automobiles, airplanes, and ships are characteristically different and uniquely designed for disparate applications. Likewise, a military vehicle designed for off-road is other than a sedan designed for city roads.

Likewise, the human body was designed to function in a terrestrial environment. It was not designed to function naturally in space. From science, we understand that oxygen is essential for the human body to function in its environment. Suppose a human body goes out of its environment, perhaps into an extraterrestrial environment. In that case, critical protections are imperative to sustain its functioning. This is why astronauts wear spacesuits, of which an oxygen tank is a crucial part, to protect their bodies from the dangers of being in space. Therefore, the physical realm includes terrestrial and extraterrestrial environments; it is simply anywhere the human body can adapt to function.

Our physical bodies are inseparable from our environment. The earth is the human body's primary place of existence. It is our bodies that make us physical beings. Without the body, there is no physicality. Hence when a person dies, it marks the end of their physical existence. In like manner, for a spiritual being to transition to the physical realm, a physical entity (a vessel) is needed. This was the principle in operation for Jesus Christ to come to the earth in the flesh. It is also the concept behind the indwelling of God (The Holy Spirit) within us. Likewise, the kingdom of darkness exploits this principle for demonic possession and operation.

There is a concept I would like to challenge. **Hebrews 9:27 NLT** makes it clear that when a person dies, the next thing is judgment. This truth invalidates the concept of ghosts or tormented souls roaming the earth. Unfortunately, this is an idea some people firmly hold. As per the scriptures, an individual faces immediate judgment when they die. Many have failed to understand that when a person dies, their spirit passes on; however, their bodily identity can still be hijacked by any spirit. If a spirit can possess a person while they are alive, how much more when their spirit leaves their body? Hence, a ghost is not the spirit of a dead person; it is simply the outcome of a demonic spirit (often a familiar spirit) stealing the bodily identity of a deceased person. This is especially true when an unbeliever dies; their body is more susceptible to demonic possession. This is one of many reasons behind demonic presences and activities at the cemeteries.

Jude 1:9 NLT describes a similar instance in the Bible. *"I said but even Michael, one of the mightiest of the angels, did not dare accuse the devil of blasphemy, but simply said, the Lord rebuke you!"* The dialogue here points us to an argument between Angel Micheal and the devil over Moses' body. You may wonder why the devil was bent on taking Moses' body. Toward the end of Moses' life, he sinned against God (**Numbers 20**). As such, the devil was convinced he had claimed the rights to his body like every other sinner. Moses was a man of great anointing and stature. A body like that would have been a great asset to the devil for manipulation. The anointing that God released upon Moses remained in his body. Moses died, and his spirit left to face judgment, yet the devil contended for his body. For those who are not saved, the devil can easily assume their physical identity at any time.

Another instance we can recount is found in **2 Kings 13:21**, where the Prophet Elisha's bones raised the dead. Such instances demonstrate that the gifts of God are irrevocable (**Romans 11:29**). Every anointing released by God remains in the physical forever.

Do you know that while people are alive, their bodies can be used by demons or borrowed by God? You may have heard or even experienced seeing the image of your pastor or spiritual authority in a dream or vision; this is because God will sometimes use this medium to communicate truth to His children. Sometimes all it takes is a familiar face for us to trust what God is saying. For example, In **Genesis 18:2-3**, Abraham saw three men and ran to meet them. Similarly, Lot saw two of the same men Abraham had seen earlier and reacted in the same way (**Genesis 19:1-2**). Both Abraham and Lot used the salutation "my Lord." We know Abraham and Lot were related; I am inclined to believe that these men came in a familiar form known to both Abraham and Lot. If God shows up in His majesty, His help might not be received. So, Jesus had to leave His glory to be born as a regular man (**Philippians 2:5-8**). Hence, God may borrow the identity of a willing servant we know and trust to speak to us. On the flip side, the devil uses this method as well.

As I have mentioned earlier, God is spirit. We must also remember that the devil was initially created as a heavenly being (**Isaiah 14:12**). He was an angel, thus existing primarily in the spirit realm. This makes him a spiritual being. Per the scriptures, man was the only creature with a dual nature—spiritual and physical. Therefore, a physical entity is required for God or the devil to operate in the physical realm. God is looking for vessels (you and I) to use and reward (**Ezekiel 22:30 & 1 Timothy 5:18**); however, our willingness to surrender to Him is foremost (**Revelation 3:20**). On the other hand, the devil is also looking for vessels to occupy and destroy (**John 10:10 and 1 Peter 5:8**). **Ephesians 4:27** advises us not to give the enemy a foothold. The devil is not looking for our willingness but instead focused on our carelessness and emptiness. Therefore, we must remain vigilant (**1 Peter 5:8**).

In summary, the physical is any environment where the body can either function naturally or adapt to function.

THE SPIRITUAL

Google defines spirituality as the quality of being concerned with the human spirit or soul instead of material or physical things. First, recognize that this definition includes the soul. Though this is not entirely true, it is based on the fact that two realms are known to us. Therefore, if humans exist in both the physical and spiritual realms, we can safely conclude that the soul falls within the spiritual realm. Hence, this definition speaks to the quality of our concern for spiritual things. The intentional effort we put towards the spiritual determines the quality of our spirituality. How deliberate is our effort when it comes to spirituality? The greater our effort towards it, the greater the outcome.

The physical realm can be understood as a tangible environment where all five senses of the flesh can function. It is a similar case for the spiritual realm. It is an environment where the spirit functions. Therefore, what the body is to the physical, is what the spirit is to the spiritual.

Why is the spiritual realm not recognized as much if humans exist in two realms? This is because the human race has only partially acknowledged the spiritual realm. Even though science has alluded to the spiritual realm by indicating that there is more to this world than what meets the eye, it has failed to explain spiritual things. It is rather inclined toward trivializing spiritual things using various physical philosophies. The truth is, we all know a greater power exists outside of our physical world. That power is the Almighty God. In my opinion, beliefs that declare there is no God have no sensible backing (**Psalm 14:1**). Yes, one may shoot down their inner intuition and give their mind over to a satisfying physical philosophy. But, the Bible speaks an unchanging truth; *God has planted eternity (an unending realm—spirituality) in the human heart* (**Ecclesiastes 3:11 NLT, emphasis added**). It is embedded in our being to acknowledge the Great I Am; however, human's free will to make choices can be a hindrance.

Ecclesiastes 3 points us to a significant difference between the physical and the spiritual. In the physical realm, things have a date of expiration. By the will of God and His timing, the world as we know it will one day come to an end (**Matthew 24:6-14**). Though the date and time are unknown to man (**Matthew 24:36**), the end will undoubtedly come. Because man primarily exists in this realm, we are not exempt from this. **Hebrews 9:27** helps us to understand that there is an appointed time for everyone to die. The arrival of this time marks our end in the physical realm.

On the other hand, the spiritual is eternal. This means there is no end or expiry date. We exist there now and will continue to exist after this physical life ends. As we will see in the next topic, our spirit is needed to exist in the physical. However, we do not need our body to exist in the spiritual (**1 Corinthians 15:52**). Our spirit keeps us alive physically. Therefore, how we grow in the spiritual, while we live in the physical, will shape our spirituality even in the afterlife. Based on these facts, spirituality is the most important.

Since God and the devil primarily exist in the spiritual, it is wise not to ignore or wander aimlessly into this realm. Good and evil emanates from the spiritual realm. God operates on the side of goodness, while the devil operates on the side of evil. This is because there are so many spirits—good and evil on each side.

For the children of God to commune with their Father and the children of the devil to commune with the devil, a connection must be established in the spiritual. The Bible said in **John 4:24 NLT** that "*God is Spirit, so those who worship him must worship in spirit and in truth.*" Similarly, "*the devil is spirit, so those that worship him must worship in spirit and in lies.*" To communicate in this spiritual realm, one must see, hear and perceive beyond the physical. A person without an understanding of how to access the spiritual realm will always be subject to those who do. Hence, a spiritually awakened person is superior to anyone functioning at the physical level. Our experience here on earth will be great if we can come alive spiritually. It might take some time, but we are headed for greatness in the physical and spiritual afterlife (**Isaiah 3:10**).

God does not need a human vessel to function in the spiritual realm, nor does the devil, because it is their natural habitat. However, when it comes to manifesting on the earth (the physical realm), both God and the devil need a human vessel or representative. But before anything can gain expression or be manifested in the physical realm, it must first be established in the spiritual realm. The case of Job validates this (**Job 1:6 & 2:1**); before he was attacked physically, a deal was already sanctioned spiritually.

Despite these critical aspects of spirituality, one of the reasons that the realm of the spirit is unpopular is tied to an event in the beginning (**Genesis 3**). Adam and Eve disobeyed God—i.e., they sinned. In accordance with **Romans 6:23**, *the wage of sin is death*. After Adam and Eve sinned, the Bible made us understand that they were still physically alive. We can say they became more aware of the physical (**Genesis 3:7**). Superficially, this appears to be incongruous with what Romans 6:23 tells us about the wages of sin. In reality, this is what happened. If we are not alive to God in the spiritual, then we are dead to Him and alive to sin. Being alive to sin is to be more aware of the physical and thereby a slave to the devil in the spiritual (See **Romans 8**). The first people died spiritually in God and became more aware of the physical (i.e., alive to sin). Before the fall, Adam and Eve's connection to God was alive and active. After the fall, their connection to God was lost; the very link that sustained their spiritual life was severed (**Romans 8:16**). Remember, in the physical, we experience life because of the breath of God (**Genesis 2:7**). Similarly, we experience life in the spiritual as a result of our connection to God.

Sin robbed Adam and Eve of the ability to connect with God. When God made them, He created them to be alive to Him in the spiritual. This is why they could easily commune with God and why God came to them in the cool of the day (**Genesis 3:8**). However, after they sinned, they were forced to hide from God. Because when a person is dead spiritually, they will always live in fear. Fear is a sign of death to God spiritually.

On the other hand, faith in God is a sign of life, spiritually. Fear creates a loophole that the devil can capitalize on. This is one of many reasons Jesus came to rescue us. Hence, anyone without Jesus as their Lord and savior is dead spiritually. According to **John 4:24**, such a person cannot claim to serve God.

Another reason the realm of the spirit is unpopular pertains to physical focus. Due to the sin of the first people, we are consequently inclined to concentrate solely on the physical if our lives are void of Christ. As an enslaved person in the spiritual (**Romans 6:20**), our body must conform to what the devil dictates. Therefore, focusing on the physical is the devil's strategy to steal, kill and destroy our spiritual connection to God (**John 10:10**). Every one of us was dead to God from birth (**Romans 5:17**). Hence, the god of this world (**2 Corinthians 4:4**), of whom we are a slave to in the spiritual, will naturally have our attention in the physical (**Romans 7:15**).

However, through Jesus, we have a chance to spiritually fight for life in God, even though we are currently alive in the body (**Romans 7:25**). With the help of the Spirit of Grace—the Holy Spirit, we are strengthened to stand. When we engage in the spiritual exercises as directed by Him, we stay alive and remain spiritually in shape in God.

Many Christians struggle between realms—spiritually alive to God but still bound by sin. Like Apostle Paul (**Galatians 5:17**), absolute freedom from slavery is a process. It does take time, but it can be expedited through our obedience to the Holy Spirit. We must understand that the area we are most focused on will eventually win our attention (**Galatians 6:8**).

In summary, spirituality is the environment where spirits function and operate. As humans, we already exist in the spiritual as enslaved persons or an enslaver. To maximize our potential as children of God, we must engage our spirit with God's Spirit.

Finally, there are rankings and heights in the spiritual realm. To achieve healthy spiritual development, there are protocols/principles to follow. In other words, laws govern the spiritual. The good and evil that we see on earth today result from some of the rules. The intent of this book is not to frighten us but to reveal the simplicity of spiritual principles. We would learn how to implement the right laws to experience growth. I pray you get revived, remain plugged in, and spiritually grow in God while here on the earth in Jesus' name. Amen.

The Triune Nature

Previously, I slightly explained the nature of humans. However, it is vital that we thoroughly delve deeper to gain more understanding.

The genesis of human existence was spoken in **Genesis 1:26,** "*Let us make man in our image, after our likeness .*" These words indicate that God was conversing with other beings. But who was God speaking to?

We find the answer to this question in **2 Corinthians 13:14**. In concluding his letter to the Corinthians, Apostle Paul referred to three Beings in his closing remarks "*May the grace of the Lord Jesus Christ, the love of God, and the fellowship of the Holy Spirit be with you all.*" The Father, The Son, and The Holy Spirit were referred to in this scripture. Therefore, we can conclude that God spoke to Jesus, the Son and the Holy Spirit in **Genesis 1:26**.

Now let us trace these three Beings and try to connect them. So far, we have seen God in our discussions. He made man in the beginning, as we established previously. He is the God that was referred to in **Genesis 1:1 NLT** (*in the beginning, God created the heavens and the earth*). Yes, He made it all, including humans. But another character was referred to in the next verse, **Genesis 1:2 NLT**. The Bible said *the Spirit of God was hovering over the surface of the waters.* We know God is holy (**1 Peter 1:16** & **Psalm 22:3**); therefore, we can say the Spirit of God is holy. Hence the name the Holy Spirit used by Apostle Paul. So, the Spirit of God is the Holy Spirit. The last Being mentioned was Jesus Christ. As per **John 1:14**, "*the Word of God became flesh and dwelt in our midst.*" Jesus was the only divine Being that ever dwelled among humans as a man. Therefore, every Word of God is Jesus personified. God spoke creation into existence; this means that Jesus was present at creation; hence the scripture in **John 1:3** and **Colossians 1:16** is infallible.

Due to the nature of Jesus as the Word, most of His physical appearances in the old testament were implicit. For example, during the dispensation of the old testament, He was referred to in numerous prophecies (The Word of God) about the future (**Isaiah 9**). But whenever God spoke, it was Jesus (The Word) being manifested. However, there was an event that made His presence more apparent in the old testament. We can find this account in **Daniel 3:25 NKJV** when the three Hebrew boys got into trouble for standing for God. The king at the time, who was an unbeliever, said, *"Look!" he answered, "I see four men loose, walking in the midst of the fire; and they are not hurt, and the form of the fourth is like the Son of God."* Let's zoom into the last part; you will agree that saying the Son of God is an interesting choice of Word. What made an unbelieving king think God had a Son? The king saw something beyond the ordinary. He must have thought, "this is God in the form of a man." Therefore, he coined the phrase "the Son of God." However, how did we know this was Jesus? This phrase was subsequently used on several occasions to characterize Jesus. For instance, in **1 John 4:10 & 1 John 5:10**, the Bible referred to Jesus as the Son of God. Furthermore, when the demons pleaded for their lives in **Mark 5:7, Matthew 8:29** and **Luke 8:28**, they called Jesus the Son of God. These are confirmations that Jesus is indeed the Son of God.

From our study, all three beings referred to by Apostle Paul were indeed connected. From biblical studies, it is apparent that these Beings are God in their rights. They operate in the same calibre, which makes them God. To better understand this, I implore you to read the gospels (i.e., Matthew, Mark, Luke and John) and the Acts of the Apostles. The gospels affirm Jesus as God, and the Acts of the Apostles prove the Holy Spirit. Other great resources that can further your understanding are the books I authored, "The Person You Should Know" and "The Most Important Person of Our Time."

In Christendom, the word "trinity" refers to God. This is because God is a triune being. He is God and expresses His

Lordship through Jesus and the Holy Spirit. **Genesis 1:26** also demonstrates how the triune nature of God functions as one. From this scripture, we can imagine God saying, *"let us come as one and join forces to recreate the same system we have in one being."* When we connect these dots, we see that man was also created to be triune; we will explore this next.

THE HUMAN NATURE

Just as God has a triune makeup (Father, Son, and Spirit), the human being is composed of three parts; body, soul, and spirit. Together, these three parts characterize humans as both physical and spiritual beings.

To explain human nature, we must understand the elements that make up a human. Spirituality becomes frustrating when we don't understand the "why" behind the triune nature of humans. So now let us dissect each part of our triune nature and locate the why.

The Body

We have established that a physical vessel is needed to function in the physical realm. The body is the primary vessel used in the physical realm. God made the body from the dust of the earth (**Genesis 2:7**); this makes the earth the most conducive for the body. In other words, the body is programmed for the physical realm and specifically for the earth. The body is needed to experience the world tangibly. Any experience outside the confines of the earth requires that the body be protected. We cease to exist in the physical realm when the body dies.

The Spirit

We previously established that God is Spirit (**John 4:24**). The realm of the spirit, where He primarily dwells, existed before the world took its physical form. The triune Beings were in existence and present before the conversation in **Genesis 1:26**. Since God is the maker of all, we can deduce that He existed and formed the spiritual beings of the spiritual world before the physical.

Genesis 2:7 records the body being brought to life "*He (God) breathed the breath of life into the man's nostrils, and the man became a living person.*" This scripture demonstrates something interesting about the human spirit. Today, we have talented artists who have sculpted creative pieces that leave one in awe. The difference between God making a man out of the dust of the earth and an artist sculpting clay is what the Bible tells us in **Genesis 2:7**. God can breathe one breath, and life is released. An artist cannot bring a statue of clay to life. If it were possible for a man to give this kind of life, no man would ever die physically again. Death is a result of the spirit leaving the body. In other words, the moment the breath of God leaves the body, the body resumes its lifeless state. Only God has the power to create a spirit. When He breathed life into Adam, He deposited a spirit in him that brought about life (**John 6:63**). Therefore, man's spirit was contained in God before his physical body was created. God did not just make the spirit of man after completing the body. He deposited what was already made into what was just made.

God told Jeremiah in **Jeremiah 1:5 NLT**, "*I knew you before I formed you in your mother's womb. Before you were born, I set you apart and appointed you as my prophet to the* *nations*." We can interpret this as before God knits us together in our mother's womb (**Psalm 139:13**), our life (spirit) already existed in Him.

It is mind-blowing to think that you and I existed before our physical bodies took form. However, our spiritual life began when the breath of God was placed in our body (**Genesis 2:7**).

As humans, the spirit is an essential part of our being. Without the spirit, the body has no life and no purpose. We are only alive in the body because our spirit (the breath of life) is still in us. Secondly, to connect with God, who is Spirit, we need a spirit that comes from Him. When God's Spirit joins with our spirit, it affirms that we are His children (**Romans 8:16**). Communing with God is impossible without the spirit. In the spiritual realm, our representation and identification card are our spirits.

The Soul

Why do we need a soul? What purpose does it serve?

Without the soul, there would be a significant gap in the nature of man. When the Spirit of God joins with our spirit, we are connected to God (**Romans 8:16**). But what connects our body to our spirit? How does our body engage and translate spiritual experiences? The answer is the soul. The soul is what establishes the connection between our spirit and body. It serves as the bridge and interpreter between our spirit and our body. We can think of the soul as the central processing unit. The flow of information between the spiritual and physical realms is bi-directional; the soul enables communication and interpretation between both realms. Hence the soul plays a unique role. When we sleep and have encounters (e.g., dreams), our soul is the system that records the details of the encounter. When we sleep, our physical body is in a state of rest. What sustains our life in this state is our spirit. Our soul, however, remains active in processing and storing information.

The soul's function led to the command in **Philippians 4:8 NLT**, "*fix your thoughts on what is true, and honourable, and right, and pure, and lovely, and admirable. Think about things that are excellent and worthy of praise.*" The essence of this scripture is to be sensitive to what we store in our minds. Our soul will filter and interpret what our spirit or body is saying based on its content. In other words, our soul takes information, filters it and stores it in its database. Therefore, *everything is pure to those whose hearts (souls) are pure. Nothing is pure to the corrupt and unbelieving people, because their minds and consciences are polluted with immoral things.* (**Titus 1:15 NLT, emphasis added**).

The spiritual gifts we receive result from the content stored in our souls. Likewise, the gifts we don't partake in are also a result of what we have stored in our souls. For instance, faith comes from the Holy Spirit within us (**1 Corinthians 12:9**), but we only begin to enjoy the personal benefits of faith when we feed our soul with faith-building content, such as the word of God, words of encouragement, and testimonies. Therefore, *faith comes from hearing, that is, hearing the Good News about Christ* (**Romans 10:17 NLT**). Otherwise, fear is inevitable.

The soul is the central line of the human system. Yes, the spirit is who we are because this is who God sees us as. But it is the soul that will be judged in the last days. This is why Jesus implores us to take good care of our souls in **Mark 8:36** and also why salvation is for the lost souls.

In death or rapture, our bodies remain on the earth. When we die, our bodies are buried in the ground. During rapture, we will be transformed (**1 Corinthians 15:52**). This is because that which is of the earth remains on the earth. The spirit is our representation in the spiritual realm; hence once we stop existing in the body, our spirit envelopes our soul for judgment.

The content of our subconscious is rooted in our soul's depth. Therefore, "*The human heart (soul) is the most deceitful of all things, and desperately wicked. Who knows how evil it is?*" (Jeremiah 17:9 NLT, emphasis added).

As children of God, we desire to please and obey God (**John 10:27, John 14:15 & Romans 8:14**). The soul has a crucial role to play. For us to obey God, we need faith. Therefore, *it is impossible to please God without faith* (**Hebrews 11:6 NLT**). Now, what is faith? As per **Hebrews 11:1 NLT**, "*faith shows the reality of what we hope for; it is the evidence of things we cannot see.*" Faith is simply the opposite of fear. We see in **2 Timothy 1:7 NLT** that *God has not given us a spirit of fear and timidity but of power, love, and self-discipline.* A combination of these three spirits is the spirit of faith. Also, three faculties enable the soul to perform its duties; they include the *will, emotion and intellect.* Let us take a closer look at each aspect of the soul from the lens of the spirit of faith.

The Will

From **2 Timothy 1:7**, the first spirit given to us is power. Its correspondence in the soul is the will. There is a famous saying, "where there is a will, there is a way." Without willpower, action will not be taken, and decisions cannot be made. Often to get things done, we must stand on our convictions. Otherwise, we will fail to accomplish the ventures we aim to complete. God has given us a spirit of power to get things done (**2 Timothy 1:7**). However, knowing the capacity God has placed in us is key to our soul, impacting both the physical and spiritual realms.

To help our understanding, let's examine Apostle Peter. He denied Jesus three times. In one instance, Peter denied Jesus after being confronted by a servant girl (**Matthew 26:69**). But when He received the baptism of the Holy Spirit (**Acts 2:3**), his willpower was awakened, and his soul processed things with new vitality. As a result, this same Apostle preached the gospel, and 3,000 souls were added to the church in one day (**Acts 2**).

Peter had a will hence his statement in **Matthew 26:35**. We also have a will, but we often lack the power needed to back up our will. This is why when we set our minds to do something, we sometimes need help following through. The execution of a task *is not by force nor by strength, but by the Spirit of God, says the LORD of Heaven's Armies* (**Zechariah 4:6 NLT**). When the Spirit of God connects with our spirit, our soul, aided by the word (**Romans 10:17**), translates the power of the Holy Spirit to fuel our will. We have an audacity of faith (**Acts 1:8**). A will that is not driven by the word of God and empowered by the Holy Spirit is stubborn (i.e., a hardened heart). The devil powers such a will.

The Emotion

As per **2 Timothy 1:7**, the next faculty is love, and its correspondence in the soul is emotion.

Emotions are crucial because of the impact they have on the soul. Many people process information based on the wrong feelings in their souls. However, when God's love is stored in the soul, it alleviates frustration and brings peace. This kind of love is what helps us to obey God because it is the fulfilment of God's law (**Romans 13:10**).

This is the love that Jesus defined in **Mark 12:30-31 NLT**. "*And you must love the Lord your God with all your heart, all your soul, all your mind, and all your strength.' The second is equally important: 'Love your neighbour as yourself.' No other commandment is greater than these.*" This is the emotional aspect of the soul. Experiencing love in the order God has ordained helps us set our priorities right. We love God first, above all, then ourselves and, equally, our neighbours. Such a structure guarantees emotional stability, and God will be pleased.

The Intellect

From **2 Timothy 1:7**, the third faculty is self-discipline, and its correspondence in the soul is the intellect.

The third faculty of the soul espouse intellectual soundness. Self-discipline is the foundation of harnessing intellectual strength, or what the scripture describes as a sound mind.

1 Corinthians 2:16 NLT tells us, "*but we understand these things, for we have the mind of Christ.*" Our standard of self-discipline determines how like-minded we are with Christ. One of the ways we train this faculty is by studying to show ourselves approved unto God as workmen who aren't ashamed but can interpret the word of truth correctly

(2 Timothy 2:15 KJV). Giving our mind and ear to the word of God in search of God's standard is the only way to think like God. The soul becomes more effective in processing what is right when we consistently discipline ourselves to feed on God's word. To be valuable vessels in God's hand, we must have a sound mind to process His will and act on it. God will always give us enough information to put us into action. We must discipline ourselves to take action because God will never move us beyond our level of self-discipline. Therefore, a person without self-control is like a city with broken-down walls (**Proverbs 25:28 NLT**). The accuracy of our obedience to God starts from here. Without discipline, the devil will overwhelm the mind with lies; hence when information is processed, it is laced with lies. For more understanding, I encourage you to read "A Discipline Life by Emmanuel Adewusi."

Carnality, Flesh and Sin

Another term you may be familiar with from the scripture is flesh or carnality, which refers to the physical. The flesh is the body, designed to function in carnality. Carnality can also be defined as the physical or worldly environment. The distinction between the body and the spirit is that the spirit is made in God, so it will naturally want to please God. However, the body is of the earth and will not naturally want to please God. Apostle Paul explains the on-going war between the flesh and the spirit in **Galatians 5:17 NKJV**. "*For the flesh lusts against the Spirit, and the Spirit against the flesh; and these are contrary to one another, so that you do not do the things that you wish.*" Hence physical desires will always be of the earth—and will oppose what the Spirit of God desires. *The sinful nature is always hostile to God. It never did obey God's laws, and it never will* (**Romans 8:7** NLT). All the flesh desires to do is to selfishly please the body and pollute the temple the Spirit of God dwells in (**1 Corinthians 3:16**). Every command or principle of the Spirit will always frustrate the body.

Spirituality: The Good and The Bad

There are two sides to the coin when discussing spirituality: the good and the bad. **Luke 18:19** clearly states that only God is good. However, this statement raises the question: If God is good and the creator of the spiritual realm, how was evil (the bad) able to become a part of the spiritual realm?

Before God created the physical that led to man's creation, God populated the spiritual realm. This we know because according to **Colossians 1:16** NLT, emphasis added *that God created everything in the heavenly realms (spiritual) and on earth (the physical). He made the things we can see and can't see— such as thrones, kingdoms, rulers, and authorities in the unseen world (the spiritual).* Therefore, many aspects of the spiritual realm are unknown to us in the physical.

There are other beings in the spiritual. In **Revelations 4:10**, the Bible introduced us to 24 Elders in heaven. **Revelations 4:6** reveals four living beings. What these beings are, we don't know. However, we know several places in the scripture where angels are mentioned (**Revelations 8:2**).

The good nature of God helps us to know that everything God created is good (**Genesis 1:31**). We can safely say that the spiritual realm was good at the beginning when God made it. So, how did evil or "the bad" come to be?

From the prophetic revelations of Isaiah, Ezekiel, and others, we understand that the devil, the custodian of the bad, was initially created as an angel—one of the good. In **Isaiah 14:12-15,** Prophet Isaiah spoke under the Holy Spirit's inspiration and pronounced doom on the king of Babylon, who the devil had influenced. "*How you have fallen from heaven, O shining star, son of the morning! You have been thrown down to the earth, you who destroyed the nations of the world. For you said to yourself, 'I will ascend to heaven and set my throne above God's stars. I will preside on the mountain of the gods far away in the north. I will climb to the highest heavens and be like the Most High.' Instead, you will be brought down to the place of the dead, down to its lowest depths.*"

The king of Babylon exhibited the same trait that resulted in the devil's fall eons ago. Therefore, God was giving insight into what happened to the devil then and what would happen to the king of Babylon if He continued in his ways. In the same vein, God reminded the devil, who had possessed the Babylonian king, of his mishaps.

From this scripture, we know that the other name for the devil was "shining star;" this was when he was still on the Lord's side. His name is rendered Lucifer in other translations. God created the devil with good intentions and for a purpose connected to His kingdom. But pride came before the enemy's fall. The biggest mistake was the devil competing and comparing himself to God. He wanted to be like God. "'*I will climb to the highest heavens and be like the Most High, he said. Therefore, there was war in heaven. Michael and his angels fought against the dragon and his angels. And the dragon lost the battle, and he and his angels were forced out of heaven. This great dragon—the ancient serpent called the devil, or Satan, the one deceiving the whole world—was thrown down to the earth with all his angels."* **Revelation 12:7-9 NLT.**

This historical battle marked the beginning of the dark side of spirituality. Before Lucifer's fall, everything in the spiritual realm was godly and good. Due to the devil's selfish ambition, he and his co-conspirators were cast out of God's presence. The devil became the highest of the evil side (hence the name d-evil). In contrast, the co-conspirators became the agents of darkness and evil.

A new dwelling was made for the devil and his cohort. **Matthew 25:41 NLT** demonstrates this, *"Then the King will turn to those on the left and say, 'Away with you, you cursed ones, into the eternal fire prepared for the devil and his demons."* This place is what we know as hell. Hell is not for humans; however, any human intimate with the devil has made themselves a candidate for hell.

We must also understand that every creature of hell is a spiritual being. Though they were cast out of heaven, they still exist and operate primarily in the spiritual. The devil and his agents still possess the skills God gave them when they were created. This is because God does not revoke the gifts He has given (**Romans 11:29 NLT**). This means that the devil and his agents still have some of the giftings, talents, and abilities given to them by God. For example, when Prophet Ezekiel lamented over the king of Tyre, under the inspiration of God, he revealed some excellent qualities that God implanted in the devil during creation (**Ezekiel 28**). So, the bad side of spirituality is filled with many gifts, talents and abilities. This is also because the devil works tirelessly to pervert many good things God created by making counterfeits.

With this understanding, we see that spiritual growth in God is possible, just as spiritual development in demonic activity is possible. It is up to us to decide which side of the spectrum we want to develop our spirituality.

Chapter 2

Come Alive

Spiritual death is a reality for every human due to the sin of Adam and Eve (the first people). Therefore, *I was born a sinner— yes, from the moment my mother conceived me* (**Psalm 51:5 NLT**).

We are the only beings God created in His image and likeness (**Genesis 1:26**). In the eyes of our Father, we are unique and peculiar. No wonder the psalmist boldly declared, "*I am fearfully and wonderfully made; Marvelous are Your works, and that my soul knows very well*" (**Psalm 139:14 NKJV**).

1 John 4:8 helps us understand that God is Love. The depth of God's love can be seen in the details of His creation (**Genesis 2:7**). God was intentional when He created man, so much so that He invited Jesus and the Holy Spirit to take part in how man was crafted (**Genesis 1:26**). God created us in His image and likeness to lavish us with His love. We were made by Love to be loved. Beloved, let this truth always resound in your heart.

Therefore, the love of God is the premise for everything that God has done, will do, and is doing for us. The most excellent demonstration of love was when the Father sent His only Son, Jesus, to die for us (**Romans 5:8 NLT**).

Though sometimes it might seem like God doesn't love us, He sees the end from the beginning, giving Him a different perspective and approach.

When the first people sinned, God made it His mission to restore us to Himself. He intended to revive us spiritually. Remember, we connect to God through our spirit (**John 4:24**). Hence our spirit must be reconnected to God if we are to commune with Him.

Through Biblical history, we see God working to restore us to Himself. In the old testament era, people took ritualistic measures before approaching God. However, in this era, we have a new entry point into the presence of God. Why the change in the approach?

Differences in Approach

Our approach to the presence of God had to change and align with the advancement of man. Notwithstanding, God Himself remains unchanged (**Malachi 3:6**).

History teaches us that every decade goes through an advanced process. Decade after decade, the human race continues to evolve in understanding. From the time of ships to air travel, our knowledge of transportation has evolved. Humans categorize each era based on significant inventions or events, such as the stone age, industrial age, information age, etc. However, this is not indicative that God changes (**Number 23:19**). This means that God, in His infinite mercies, releases insight according to our level of understanding and the evolution of that understanding (**Isaiah 28:10**). From the old testament to this new redemptive era of

Christ, there has always been one approach to going before God. We start in the outer court, move to the inner court, and proceed to the holy of holies.

In the same way today, we come through Jesus, receive the Holy Spirit and spend eternity with the Father. God designed it so we can benefit the most from it. He reveals increments of wisdom that the people of a specific time can comprehend.

God's redemption plan was conceived right after the sin of the first people (**Genesis 3:15**). But only came to pass after more than sixty generations. There was an appointed time for humanity to be brought back to their Father this way. God programmed this time to account for our advancement in understanding. In returning to our first love through Jesus, we must come to understand the depth and mystery of God's love for humanity (**John 3:16 & Romans 5:8**). Before the dispensation of Jesus Christ, our understanding of God's love was skewed.

God gave the children of Israel many commandments, but Jesus zoomed in on one commandment of love (**Matthew 22:36-40 and Mark 12:30-31**). With the commandment of love, we fulfil all the other laws (**Romans 13:10**). Though the commandment of love is not new (**Leviticus 19 and Deuteronomy 6:5**), it was the focus of God's plan. But the people of the Old Testament could not fathom the commandment of love as the governing command. They were incapable of fulfilling it without the guardrails of the other laws in the old testament. We see that God is not reinventing the wheel (**Matthew 5:17**). Instead, He is uncovering His plans, *precept upon precept, line upon line,* for our comprehension (**Isaiah 28:10 ESV**). In the old covenant, God gave a variation of His redemptive plan that the people of that time would understand. These were only in anticipation and preparation for "the Way" (**John 14:6**).

Finally, we can fulfil all the laws today through the commandment of love (**Romans 13:10**) and the guardrail called the Holy Spirit (**John 14:15-18**).

The Approach Today

Like every parent, God wants the best for all His children (**Matthew 7:11**), and the truth is that the best can only be found in God. Therefore, it is essential to God that we are in Him to get His best for us. As per the Bible, we are only living beings because of the breath of God (**Genesis 2:7**). Therefore, as long as we are alive, the breath of God is in us. This breath will always long for God, leaving a void in each one of us—the supernatural consciousness (**Ecclesiastes 3:11**).

Adam and Eve realized this void and hid when God came to visit (**Genesis 3:8**). When we fail to fill this void with God, our life will not produce the right results. Humanity's most significant challenges began when sin appeared in the garden of Eden. Unfortunately, many people fill this void with everything but God. Neither money, career, relationships, business, nor pleasure, can compare to the fulfillment derived from being sold out to God through Jesus. Until this void is filled with God and God remains our sole focus, God's intention for overall success in every aspect of our lives will never be realized (**John 10:10**).

Whatever or whoever occupies the void becomes our focus. The results we see and experience are a product of our focus. God designed you and me to focus on one thing—**Matthew 6:33** makes it very clear. "*Seek (focus on)* *the Kingdom of God above all else, and live righteously, and he will give you everything you need"* (Emphasis added). As we excel in our pursuit of God's kingdom, God takes care of every other aspect of our lives. Thereby giving us overall success.

As we have previously discussed, every access point to God was in preparation and anticipation for "the Way"—Jesus (**Acts 22:4**). The commandments in the old testament dispensation imposed punishments and warranted sacrifices when violated. This avenue to God requires sacrifices and, as such, priests. The people had an extensive list of instructions to follow. But, in the redemptive era of the New Testament, Jesus became our sacrifice. On the cross, He paid it all once and for all (**Hebrews 7:27 and Hebrews 10**). He gave one instruction that fulfills all others—the commandment of love (**Mark 12:30-31**). He became our High Priest forever (**Hebrews 4:14**). The appearance of Jesus swallowed up every other way by bringing God's heart and intention to fruition. Jesus is not "a way" but "the Way." This was why Jesus said in **Matthew 5:17 NLT**, *Don't misunderstand why I have come. I did not come to abolish the law of Moses or the writings of the prophets. No, I came to accomplish their purpose.* The accomplishment of a purpose signifies its completion. Therefore, Jesus is the final destination to reconcile us back to God. Every other way became obsolete when Jesus died and was resurrected. Therefore, the only way to God today is through Jesus.

THE WAY: JESUS

If advancement is a present and continuous experience, how are we sure there will not be another "way" after Jesus? So how does Jesus, a man who died many years ago, lead us back to God today? Furthermore, how does all this reconnect our spirit to God?

Is Jesus the Last Approach?

Due to the nature of our creation, imagine all the unlocked potential we have yet to discover. Similarly, the universe is filled with many wonders that have yet to be discovered. The closer we get to God, the more we learn about the potential God has deposited in us and around us. The human body, the universe, and all God created will never cease to amaze us.

In introducing Jesus as "the way" to the world, God knew that it would take many years for the human mind to advance, to understand and accept Jesus as "the way." Jesus' coming was set for an appointed time. He arrived at the best time that would provide humanity with the best chance of salvation. Therefore, we can say that the timing of God puts into perspective the evolution of human understanding. With this understanding, we can also deduce that, in some cases, if God is not releasing something to us, there is a chance it is because the appointed time has not come. God's promises are released based on His all-knowing abilities and divine timing. Trust Him! At the right time, He will reveal Himself (**Habakkuk 2:3**).

Before Jesus' death and resurrection, the Israelites were governed by the law of Moses. This law dictated their lives. The law was the standard until Jesus came. However, there was a common theme throughout that period; it was the coming of the Messiah. In **Luke 2:25**, a man called Simeon anticipated the birth of the Messiah to rescue Israel.

The prophecies about the Messiah continued from the garden of Eden to Isaiah (the Prophet of old) and John the Baptist (who was only six months older than Jesus). It spoke of a redemptive future to come. This points us to the fact that the Messiah was a significant piece of our relationship with God the Father. We know that prophecies tell us what God is about to do. It helps us to build our faith in anticipation of God's plan. Using the most reliable resource available to us, the Bible, we see no prophecy about "any other way" after Jesus. The next game-changing event we are privy to is the release of the Holy Spirit (**John 14:16**) and rapture (**1 Corinthians 15:52**). Hence, this makes Jesus the Way to God before the end of days.

From the prophecies and promises, we know there was and still is a desperate need for the Messiah. However, is Jesus the Messiah? Yes, He is. There were so many prophecies about the Messiah that we can analyze. Prophet Isaiah affirmed Jesus as the Messiah.

1. Prophet Isaiah prophesied by the Spirit of God that a Son would be born of a virgin; he continued that it would be a sign from God (**Isaiah 7:14**). In **Luke 1:26-56**, an angel appeared to a virgin named Mary, and this prophecy was already in motion. This led to the virgin birth of Jesus Christ, which made Him the only person on earth conceived by a virgin without the involvement of a man. The advent of Jesus was a sign and was accompanied by signs. The wise men saw a star in heaven (**Matthew 2**). Another sign was caught by the shepherds in the field when angels appeared in heaven, singing praises to God (**Luke 2**). These signs

were no coincidence; they happened simultaneously to announce the birth and lead people to the birthplace of Jesus. Thus, confirming Jesus as the Messiah, that Prophet Isaiah prophesied.
2. In **Isaiah 53:4-6 & 11,** the Prophet prophesied about the death of the Messiah. He foresaw how it would happen and the suffering He would endure to rid us of our sins. This was fulfilled in **Matthew 27, Mark 15, Luke 23** and **John 19.** Details of the death of Jesus affirmed that all that happened to Him was pre-planned/predestined as per the prophecy.
3. It was recorded in **Isaiah 53:10-11** that the Messiah will not stay dead. Jesus was resurrected on the third day of His death, as per **Matthew 28.** Before Jesus' resurrection, Lazarus was raised by Jesus. Nevertheless, only Jesus was killed and rose from the grave, without any human effort, after three days. This affirms Him again as the prophesied Messiah.

Examining the words of Jesus Himself will give us further insight into His identity as the Messiah. In **John 14:6,** Jesus said *I am the way, the truth, and the life. No one can come to the Father except through me.* God the Father is the goal. We need to restore the access severed to get back to the Father. Not one Prophet, priest, judge, or king before Jesus made such a statement. Instead, those that God genuinely appointed redirected the focus to Jesus, the Messiah to come.

Jesus owned up to His identity as the Messiah. In **Matthew 5:17 NLT,** Jesus said, *"Don't misunderstand why I have come. I did not come to abolish the law of Moses or the writings of the prophets. No, I came to fulfill its purpose."* Every approach to God is simply the derivative of the law given to the Israelites. Therefore, Jesus must be a derivative of the law. Jesus produced results as intended by God through the law. He came to fulfil the law, that is, to bring its plan to reality. By doing this, Jesus became the completion of God's restoration plan.

Matthew 1:21 NLT also reveals the purpose Jesus came to accomplish. It says, *"And she will have a son, and you are to name him Jesus, for he will save his people from their sins."* This verse of the Bible shows us the reason why Jesus is different. It also shows why there is no need for another way, even if the human race keeps evolving in understanding. Jesus came to rescue us from sin. Every other way before, Jesus could not afford the wage of sin once and forever. However, the death and resurrection of Christ paid for it all. Therefore, there is no need for any other way to repeat what Jesus has already done.

How is Jesus the Way?

The Bible makes it clear that throughout Jesus' life, there was no sin in Him (**2 Corinthians 5:21**). He did no wrong. He was honest to His core, pure and faultless in all His ways. Therefore, His statement in **John 14:6** is trustworthy.

There are people today still waiting on the promises of the Messiah. Suggesting that the Messiah must be the only way; without Him, humanity is doomed. The significance of the coming of the Messiah cannot be emphasized enough. The Israelites understood this firsthand from their experience in Egypt. God promised to send them a deliverer to rescue them from slavery. God sent Moses on that assignment as the fulfillment of His promise to the Israelites.

Their freedom only came as a result of Moses' response to the calling of God over his life. Without Moses, there might have been no deliverance.

In the same way, the promise of the Messiah was and still is the only hope we have in a life free from sin and death. Though the interpretation of freedom varied at different points in time, it was clear that a savior was needed. **John 1:17 NLT** explains that *the law was given through Moses, but God's unfailing love and faithfulness came through Jesus Christ*. Again, this scripture affirmed Jesus Christ as the deliverer sent to go beyond what Moses did. If Jesus is the Messiah, and the Messiah is the only way to God, then Jesus is the only way to God.

In **Isaiah 53**, we read that the Messiah must carry away our sins. The primary reason behind our loss of connection to God was sin. The Bible explicitly states that God cannot stand sin. He hates sin (**Psalm 5:4**). For the Messiah to reconnect us back to God, He must first take away our past and present sins; then create a preventive measure against future sin. Jesus paid the price for our past and present sins and our future mistakes when He died on the cross (**John 1:29**). He had to die to fulfill scripture. According to **Hebrews 9:22 NLT**, *without the shedding of blood, there is no forgiveness*. When He died, He went to hell to reclaim everything that was stolen from us in the beginning. In His resurrection, He claimed victory (**Matthew 28:18**), symbolizing the defeat of sin, death and Satan. He reclaimed the power that was forfeited in the garden of Eden. Therefore, the moment we come to Christ, we are restored to our rightful place of freedom and authority as children of God.

Jesus is the way because He revives our spirit. He did this when He opened the door for the Holy Spirit. In **John**

16:7, Jesus told the disciples that He should leave to create a portal for the Holy Spirit. How? Our spirit is what became dead to God. However, the death and resurrection of Jesus make it possible for the Holy Spirit to dwell in us and with us. The Holy Spirit is a very holy Being, and we are sinners by default (**Romans 3:23**). Therefore, the Holy Spirit cannot simply dwell with the human spirit. Until an individual rids themself of sin, the Holy Spirit cannot dwell inside them. This was why the Holy Spirit mostly came upon people in the old testament rather than dwelling within them. Conquering sin was part of Jesus' mission here on earth. Jesus, through His death and resurrection, took away our sins. In this way, He made us holy (**Hebrews 10:10**). This is the first step before we can access the Holy Spirit. Jesus made this first step possible and thereby revived our spirit.

Our Responsibilities.

So far, we have affirmed that Jesus is the Messiah, the only way to God now and forever, and through His work, our spirit is revived. However, how are we to tap into this?

Step One.

From **1 Corinthians 14:33**, we know God is of order. We also know that to enjoy anything of value, guiding principles must be followed. In the same way, connecting to God through Jesus requires that specific steps be taken. Many people have heard of Jesus; some even know everything there is to know about Him. However, the knowledge of Jesus is not enough to secure eternal life. So it is when we follow the path laid out for salvation. Remember that

Jesus is the first step to our destination—reunion with God the Father.

Jesus says in **John 10:9 NLT**, *"Yes, I am the gate. Those who come in through me will be saved. They will come and go freely and will find good pastures."* This statement signifies something interesting. In other translations, "the door" is used instead of "the gate." Both words denote "entryway"—the entryway to the Father. Hence, it is only open to everyone that enters through Jesus. Even though we come in through the door (Jesus), there are additional steps to stay inside and get to the Father, which we will discuss in the next chapter.

In accomplishing this first step, we must follow what **Romans 10:9 NKJV** outlines. Here the Bible says that *if we confess with our mouth that Jesus is Lord and believe in our heart that God has raised Him (Jesus) from the dead, we will be saved.* This verse shows that the step is to confess and believe.

Confess

Confession means to declare a belief for others to hear verbally. Confession is not a matter of the heart but that of the mouth. First, though, it must be founded in the heart (**Matthew 12:34b**). When we openly confess something, we identify with it. In our open confession of Christ, we verbalize our identity as children of God and members of His kingdom. As a result, everyone (including Satan and his demons) must know about the change. Our confession notifies all principalities of the change. In evangelical events, altar calls are made for this very reason.

The Bible tells us to confess the Lord Jesus. How do we do this? It is simply to confess our allegiance to Jesus. We confess Him as the Lord of our life. This means to acknowledge Him and all He stands for. As we have learnt, Jesus' purpose is to save us from sin (**Matthew 1:21**); therefore, when we confess Him, we must desire to give up our sins and receive His love and freedom. We relinquish our sinful nature to Him in exchange for a new identity. The Bible tells us in **1 John 1:9 NLT** (emphasis added), *"If we confess our sins to him (Jesus), he is faithful and just to forgive us our sins and to cleanse us from all wickedness."* You do not need to relive your sin; just let Him know you have given it all to Him in your confession.

Believe

Here is another crucial step, but a thing of the heart. Therefore, it is an event between the person and God. Over the years, we have seen people confess, but there was no evidence of salvation. Perhaps, they did not believe in their heart. Therefore, it is essential to understand and believe that God raised Jesus from the dead for us to stand a chance of being saved. Otherwise, confession is a waste of time. Yes, the name of Jesus and His salvation work are powerful, but without believing, it will never be adequate. If you still have challenges believing that God raised Jesus, ask questions and get understanding. This is because everything in the kingdom of God rises and falls on faith (**Hebrews 11:6**). Believing God's mighty work through Jesus is critical.

To get us to do both in one sweep, Christians have devised a simple prayer, often referred to as "the sinner's prayer." Believing is an act between a person and God. So say this simple prayer by faith and believe in your heart.

Dear heavenly Father,

I thank You for sending Your son Jesus to die on the cross for my sins. I know I am a sinner in need of a savior. I confess my sin and ask You for forgiveness. I believe that Jesus died for my sins and You raised Him up to claim my victory. I confess and accept Jesus as my personal Lord and Savior and invite Him into my heart. With your help, I will trust and obey You forever. So, help me, God, in Jesus' name. Amen

Step Two

We gain access to God when we accept Christ as Lord and Savior. Our spirit is revived, and there is an established connection between our spirit and God via our access to the Holy Spirit (**Acts 2:38**). However, as we will see in Chapter 3, this is only the first step. Jesus said He is the gate/door; no one is permitted to access God without going through Him (**John 14:6**). Therefore, when we come through Jesus, the gate/door is swung open. The light turns green, indicating our right of way. Beyond the gate is a staircase leading to God at the very top. This staircase is the next step. We can come in through Jesus and remain at the entrance, thereby short-circuiting our salvation. It is our responsibility to take the first step on this staircase. The light can be green, signalling an opportunity to move past a current standpoint. However, one must take action in faith to move beyond their current standpoint.

In the analogy above, the staircase is the Holy Spirit. Jesus left so we can have the Holy Spirit (**John 16:7**). He is the Person to whom Jesus gave us access. Once we walk through the gate/door—of Jesus, the next step is to connect with the Holy Spirit (**Luke 24:49**). Salvation gives us access to the staircase—the Holy Spirit. However, having access is not the same as being on the stairs. Once we pass through the gate, we are in God's environment but still at the entrance. To maximize our access, we must move beyond the entrance and take the first step on the staircase. The disciples had access to the Holy Spirit through Jesus (**John 20:22**). However, it was not until **Acts 2** that they engaged with the Holy Spirit in obedience to the instructions given by Jesus in **Acts 1:4-5**. Jesus said, "*Do not leave Jerusalem until the Father sends you the gift He promised. John, baptized with water, but you will be baptized with the Holy Spirit in just a few days.*"

Take the First Stairs

The disciples were new believers at this point after the death of Jesus. They had just experienced a transforming work but needed to learn how to proceed. This is a common state for many new believers. Instead of looking for a formula book of dos and don'ts, adhere to the instruction Jesus gave the disciples. After receiving salvation, do not leave the presence of God until you have connected with the gift of the Holy Spirit. Wait for the Spirit of God to come upon you (the baptism) before you leave. Even though Jesus said to wait, He did not necessarily mean to pray alone. We must ask God for the baptism of His Spirit (**Luke 11:13**), but this is not the only way to receive Him. In **Acts 2**, the disciples waited in one accord. In the case of Cornelius, the Holy Spirit fell on his household by hearing the word of God (**Acts 10**). In every instance where the baptism of the Holy Spirit was received, the recipients were willing and desired the Spirit of God. God will not force Himself on us; we must want Him ourselves. Once the desire is there, we can activate the Holy Spirit. Desire is essential. The Holy Spirit, like God, is gentle and will never force Himself on anyone (**Revelations 3:20**). If we do not desire Him, we cannot receive Him. So, right after we are saved, we must desire the baptism of the Holy Spirit.

In summary, once we come through the gate—Jesus, we have access to the staircase—the Holy Spirit (**Acts 2:38**). Consequently, we have the anointing within. This anointing is strengthened via obedience (**John 14:15**). But we engage this anointing within us to come upon us by receiving the baptism of the Holy Spirit as seen in **Acts 2:1-4** and **Acts 4:31**. Through obedience and activating the anointing upon us, we maximize our salvation and take the first step on the staircase—the Holy Spirit. For more insight, please read the book I authored, "The Most Important Person of Our Time."

Chapter 3

Stay Alive

Congratulations, now that you are alive to God in the Spirit. Your Spirit is now directly connected with the Holy Spirit, affirming that you are God's child (**Romans 8:16 & 1 Corinthians 6:17**). Using the physical body as a point of reference, we will be elucidating a few things that keep us alive physically and their interpretation in the spiritual.

When a baby is born in the physical, special care and specific procedures must be followed to keep the newborn alive. The same principle applies to the spiritual. We become newborns in God's spiritual world when we become born again. This chapter will discuss a few essential facts in the physical that may need to be emphasized more for the spiritual.

A Home

A home, according to Google, is "*a place where one lives permanently, especially as a member of a family or household.*"

The statement, "*where one lives permanently*," indicates that a home is a place with much history that marks significant milestones in one's life. Home is also famous for gathering family and loved ones together. From this definition, we can see many benefits to a home. These include a place where you can be yourself without the fear of being judged, a place where you can let your guard down, a place of rest, and a place of growth. Hence, if a home is a place of growth, then with growth comes a few unpleasant pruning. A home is also a place for discipline that shapes us to be the best versions of ourselves.

Another significant benefit of a home is shelter and safety. As per Google, shelter protects us from harmful things. These may be inclement weather, diseases, viruses and many more.

The home also serves as a base. It is usually the first place people can look for an individual when they need to be located. A good home plays a significant role in ensuring a good quality of life for any individual. Yet, In our world today, homelessness is prevalent. People experiencing homelessness find it very difficult to make headway in life because the rebuilding process appears impossible and requires a lot of time. The psychological effect of having a place of our own is beyond comprehension. This is one main reason behind adoption and foster parenting. The concept of a physical home is comparable in the spiritual sense. In Christianity, our spiritual home is the church of God. It is any church where God has placed you. In this way, everybody chosen by God to be a part of that church is your spiritual sibling, and the shepherds over that church are ideally your spiritual parents.

In the same way, a Christian without a spiritual home is spiritually homeless. For example, a person without a spiritual home may find it challenging to get some revelations from God. The reasoning behind this is that some revelations from God will be relayed to you personally. At your spiritual home, other revelations will be released via sermons, teachings, prophecies, and so forth. That is why knowing where you can call your spiritual home is vital. Just as we can't simply hop from family to family, we must avoid doing that spiritually. You don't get to choose your family; God places you in a biological family and, subsequently, a spiritual family He deems fit.

In the physical, once we grow, the normal progression of things is to move out and start our own lives and make a new home. However, this is only sometimes the case in the spiritual. We never grow beyond needing a spiritual home, regardless of our anointing. As children of God, we must belong to a spiritual home for the rest of our physical lives. Therefore, the Bible advises us *to not neglect our meeting together, as some people do, but encourage one another, especially now that the day of his return is drawing near* (Hebrews 10:25 NLT).

Starting your own home will be interpreted here as starting a church; this is not and should never be our prerogative but God's. We must remember that only God reserves the right to put us in a family and determines who gets to start a home spiritually. So, if God has not called you to shepherd, you must stay put wherever He has placed us (1 Corinthians 7:17).

Lastly, I would like to address the concept of church hopping. This is a necessity that must be addressed. I am not referring to those still unsure of where God wants them to be or still praying to find out. I am talking about those who know where they ought to be or do not want to be part of a local church. This is simply unacceptable.

Similarly, you cannot be part of the Williams family today and part of the Smiths family tomorrow, so it is in the spirit. The issue with church hopping is that it gives room for confusion instead of growth. If God has placed you in a home, all the messages and resources required for increase and development will be found there. Remember, God is not the author of confusion (**1 Corinthians 14:33**). Church-hopping is a form of spiritual homelessness that opens a person to all sorts of danger, stunted growth, and misconceptions.

Parental Care

For any newborn to stay alive, parental care is essential. No wonder parental negligence can result in the death of a baby. Understanding the concept of spiritual parenthood is critical to staying alive and growing in God's spiritual world.

In the physical, babies are generally a result of the communion between two people (a man and a woman). Under normal circumstances, one or both parties take responsibility for the newborn. A parent is any person responsible for the well-being of a newborn. Being involved in bringing about a baby (such as carrying the baby or having sexual relations) does not qualify a person as a parent; it only makes the person a vessel or a means.

Using the logic above, we can say that for every newborn (born again) Christian, God uses vessels to bring about their birth. But, just as in the physical, not every vessel can be a parent. Bringing about a newborn in the Spirit can result from a joint effort between an individual and God. That is why *there is joy in the presence of God's angels when one sinner repents* (**Luke 15:10 NLT**). For example, a lot goes into a successful evangelistic meeting. To name a few, God opens the eyes of the unbeliever so they can receive (**2 Corinthians 4:4 NLT**). However, the individual(s) leading the meeting has a role to play in ensuring they are emotionally and spiritually prepared (by fasting and praying), as well as physically prepared (by organizing the event and sacrificing their time). Evangelism is a joint venture between God and humans. For more understanding of evangelism, I recommend reading the book I authored, "The Most Important Act" and "A Skillful Sower" by Emmanuel Adewusi.

WHO IS MY SPIRITUAL PARENT?

Only some vessels can be a parent. So, who are my spiritual parents? For every work of God on earth, a human is involved. This is because God gave Adam (the first human) dominion on earth in **Genesis 1:26**, which makes the earth our domain. Therefore, under the spiritual principle, a human vessel is required for any spiritual being to operate in this domain. The moment we become born again, God becomes our Father in Heaven (See **Matthew 23:9** & **Matthew 6:9**). However, we are still on earth physically; so, if we are to stay alive in God's spirit world while on earth, then another human vessel is needed. Our spiritual birth requires a human vessel, and so does remaining alive in God's spirit world. Therefore, every genuine child of God that is alive must have a human vessel appointed by God to parent them spiritually here on earth. These vessels are called the earthly spiritual parent. The day a child of God grows beyond the parenting of any human vessel, God can take them to heaven (See **Genesis 5:24**). Nevertheless, as far as a child of God is alive here on earth, an earthly spiritual parent is needed.

As discussed, we know there are two different spiritual parents for born-again Christians; the heavenly spiritual parent and the earthly spiritual parent. Our heavenly spiritual parent is God. He is our ultimate spiritual parent because He created us and knew us even before we were born (both physically and spiritually) (See **Jeremiah 1:5**). Based on this knowledge of who we are and what we need to stay alive spiritually, God chooses our earthly spiritual parent for us. The vessel used for birth may or may not become our earthly spiritual parent. In **1 Corinthians 4:15**, the vessel was their earthly spiritual parent. Only God has the criteria to decide if the vessel will become our parent or if He will give us an adopted parent altogether (See **Jeremiah 3:15**).

As a new babe in Christ, one of the first steps we must take is to join a local church. Yes, heaven is our ultimate home when we are born again. But while we are alive here on earth, we need an earthly spiritual home, as we have explained earlier. The local church is our earthly spiritual home. In the physical, a good home consists of a parent and their children. Likewise, in the spiritual, a good home consists of a God-ordained parent and the children of God, who are fed and nurtured to grow. This is the concept behind the church being a family; everyone appointed by God to be part of that spiritual home is a sibling. Thus early believers used brother and sister salutations as a sign of mutual respect.

Therefore, we are commanded not to forsake our family (See **Hebrews 10:25**).

In the case of a spiritual home, the parent is often the shepherd over the home, that is, the Pastor of the local church. While God is the head of the church through Jesus (See **Colossians 1:18**), He appoints *shepherds after His own heart, who will guide you with knowledge and understanding* (**Jeremiah 3:15 NLT**). These shepherds function in a management capacity; they are there to manage the Church of Christ till He returns for His bride (**2 Corinthians 11:2**). These Shepherds appointed by God often become our earthly spiritual parent when we join a spiritual home. This is usually the typical approach; however, at God's discretion, He can appoint a spiritual parent that is outside the spiritual home for an individual. This is usually the case for many shepherds of a local church. These arrangements are not standard, but God has the final say. Therefore, we must always pray to God before we join a church or submit to any earthly spiritual parent.

Lastly, it is crucial to understand that just as every family in the physical is different, so is our spiritual family. Yes, as per **1 Corinthians 12:27**, we are all the body of Christ. However, we must understand that the body of Christ has different parts, each with a unique function and needs. All children of God collectively make up the body of Christ. This means that some spiritual homes and individuals may be the hand of Christ, others the legs, and so on. This metaphor does not connote superiority; it elucidates that we are destined for different things in our journey with God. Therefore, the nature of food ingested and activities undertaken by the hand of Christ's body might differ from that of the leg of Christ's body. This is why jealousy within the body is simply a lack of understanding (See **1 Corinthians 12:21**). If a person meant to be the hand ends up the leg, there would be frustration and potential stagnation. The point is that only God knows the right part of the body to which we belong. Therefore, His responsibility is to choose an earthly spiritual home and parents for us. Once we know our earthly spiritual home and parents, we must remain undercover to live and grow.

SPIRITUAL PARENT VS SPIRITUAL MENTOR

For even if you had ten thousand others to teach you about Christ, you have only one spiritual father. For I became your father in Christ Jesus when I preached the Good News to you. (1 Corinthians 4:15 NLT)

Apostle Paul here opens our eyes to something crucial. There is a difference between a parent and a mentor. Many Christians use these terms interchangeably, but this is only sometimes accurate. Only with a proper understanding of the distinction might we get the blessings associated with each of them.

A mentor, as per Google, is an experienced and trusted adviser in straightforward terms. Mentors can also be deemed as teachers because they are there to train. But a parent is responsible for our whole well-being. This is why we can only have one earthly spiritual parent but as many teachers as needed. We may require different mentors for every stage of life, but unless a spiritual parent misses their way in God, they stay with us regardless of the stages. For instance, you have a new teacher when you finish a class and advance to another. In some cases where the teacher might need to be better, you switch or drop the class. However, you are stuck with a parent unless God says otherwise.

A spiritual parent and mentor are both needed spiritually. In some cases, our parents can mentor us. First, however, we must understand their role at each point to get the best out of it. In the physical, some things will be learnt only from teachers and some from parents. For example, I had to go to school to be taught by teachers, earn a degree and have a professional career. But the lessons of life can only be taught by parents. This is the same in the spiritual.

THE RESPONSIBILITIES OF EARTHLY SPIRITUAL PARENTHOOD

Parenting means taking on responsibility and guardianship for another individual. In doing so, we must understand that spiritual parents are responsible for our well-being spiritually and any other area God has assigned them to be accountable. These affairs include anything that may affect you spiritually. God is Spirit (See **John 4:24**); He first sees things from a spiritual perspective. So, when God looks at a person, He observes them first from the standpoint of their spiritual lineage. I am not saying that the physical parent or lineage does not matter, but when it comes to spiritual things, the spiritual is more important. The physical is for physical things (**John 3:6**), and we need this to be distinguished. For example, everything that happened to Job was concluded in the spiritual before it manifested physically (See **Job 1:6 & 2:1**). We can see that if our spirituality is not adequately aligned, it can put our physical self in danger.

Our physical lineage may come into play when God is dealing with us physically (like our health). But our identity spiritually is based on our spiritual family. This is a spiritual principle that even demons understand (See **Acts 19:15**). Therefore, what a spiritual parent suffers or excels in is duplicated in their spiritual children, just as in the physical. Suppose a believer is still under the devil's oppression spiritually as a result of their physical lineage. In that case, this could be a result of a few things:

1. They may still spiritually identify with their physical lineage, knowingly or unknowingly. This is the default setting until we become saved.
2. They may not have an understanding of their freedom in Christ.
3. Their spiritual lineage suffers the same fate.

Just as parenthood is a responsibility synonymous with maturity in the physical, so is spiritual parenthood. Under normal circumstances, parents chosen for us by God are usually ahead of us spiritually; they are well-nurtured, matured and advanced in spiritual things. Therefore, we can be parented by such a person. Because they are also human, God can prompt a change quickly the day a spiritual parent stops growing. Just as in the physical, every spiritual parent must be under another spiritual parent. If you don't know your spiritual grandparent, ask! You must be able to trace your lineage or at least know that it exists. This will help you understand and know what is available to you spiritually. If your grandfather possesses something, you don't need to fight for it. It is yours by right.

Parents must understand that children are gifts from God (See **Psalm 127:3**). When we come to God through Jesus, we are connected back to God through our spirit (**Romans 8:16**), and we become a child. This means that there is a lot we do not know spiritually, regardless of our age physically. As such, the devil can still poke at other aspects of our being (soul and body). Every spiritual child will still have different negative tendencies in different areas based on their maturity. Therefore, spiritual parents have been mandated by God to raise godly spiritual Children (**Proverbs 22:6**). To get this done, the parent must be willing. The child must anticipate scolding, discipline, and anything godly that will help them grow (**Proverbs 22:15**). This is in alignment with God's style of parenting (**Hebrews 12:6** and **Proverbs 3:12**). A parent that does not engage in this is neglecting their responsibility and, as such, can be replaced. However, God frowns and does not tolerate abusive parenting, either physically or spiritually, as seen in **Ephesians 6:4** and **Colossians 3:21**.

The selection and replacement of spiritual parents are reserved for God alone. If there are any red flags, we must take them to God, who will lead us. Remember, nobody is perfect; only God is. So, when it comes to earthly spiritual parenthood, focus on your growth and staying alive. Ignore physical weaknesses unless the Spirit of God prompts you to pay attention to them. Be assured that they'll make mistakes, but God, who placed them over you, will help you. If you have any issues with your earthly spiritual parents, always go to your heavenly spiritual parent for direction; He alone has the final say on your overall well-being.

Having an earthly spiritual authority does not negate the heavenly spiritual authority. On the contrary, if you are to stay alive, your heavenly authority must precede the earthly one. Communing and developing a relationship with the heavenly authority is imperative. A God-ordained earthly spiritual parent will always refer you to the heavenly spiritual parent. Also, I will advise that at the beginning of your walk with God, go to God for everything you can think of. Do not stop until God feels that you are mature enough to handle certain things on your own. Do not assume anything;

let God be the one to tell you what you can and cannot do yourself. He wants you to call on Him (**Jeremiah 33:3**).

The sole reason for the existence of our earthly spiritual parent is to validate our heavenly spiritual parent. Therefore, it is their responsibility to interpret heaven for us. Remember, God is higher than us in every way possible (**Isaiah 55:8**). As such, we will always need an interpreter to relate to God. But as we mature, we learn more about God, and the interpretation we need decreases. Notwithstanding, until our days on earth end, we will always need an interpreter in some areas of our walk with God. Hence the need for earthly spiritual parents as long as we live. Remember, it took Jethro's advice to liberate Moses from untimely death (**Exodus 18**).

Some might argue that the Holy Spirit interprets God to us. Yes, this is true. We hear God the Father primarily through the Holy Spirit. God, the Father and the Holy Spirit are one being. As such, the Holy Spirit is our heavenly spiritual authority. God doesn't hide or try to make things hard for us (**1 Corinthians 14:33**). The issue is that God's mode of communication is too complex for us sometimes. In God's quest to relate with us, He provided us with all we may need to communicate with Him, hence an interpreter. However, the more we understand God's mode of communication, the less interpretation we will require until we leave the earth. Therefore, God may defer to earthly spiritual authority when we ask Him certain questions.

While we are alive on earth, our earthly spiritual parenthood may be our only human covering in the spiritual realm. As such, many benefits are obtainable when done right. You can read about these benefits in "The Blessings of Being Under Spiritual Authority" by Emmanuel Adewusi.

Air

Air is an essential element for our physical existence. If we are deprived of air for some time, our bodies will start shutting down. As per the rule of three, three minutes without oxygen is deadly to us. If the brain is deprived of air for some time, the damage to the brain becomes irreparable. Therefore, when air ceases in the physical, death is inevitable.

In the same way, *should we keep sinning so that God can show us more and more of his wonderful grace? Of course not! Since we have died to sin, how can we continue to live in it?* (**Romans 6:1-2 NLT**). In the spiritual, the air we breathe is God's grace. This grace is available to us once we become saved. Our spiritual health and growth are indications of the grace we have available to us. Therefore, we are alive spiritually based on the grace of God available to us (**1 Corinthians 15:10**). This was why God told Paul in **2 Corinthians 12:9** that His grace is sufficient. This means that just as physical air is sufficiently available, the grace of God is adequately available. No matter what we face or are going to face, the grace of God is more than enough. So the Bible in **Romans 5:20 NLT** said, *but as people sinned more and more, God's wonderful grace became more abundant.* Apostle Paul's case referred to earlier; we see that though this grace is available in the spiritual, the result was applicable physically. So, the air that we breathe spiritually can have an impact on us physically. This again confirms the superiority of the spiritual over the physical.

In Christianity, we use the word "grace period." As per the mercies of God, when we sin, He convicts us and gives us time to repent. This period is what we refer to as the grace period. This is the period between a person's sin and judgment. It is the time between when sin is committed and when God completely rejects a person. It is the period before a person becomes a lost course to God. It is the period of God's patience after a person has sinned (**Romans 2:4**). When we sin, the Spirit of God convicts us through our conscience, and the grace period is activated; once we repent, the grace period is deactivated. Sadly, the grace period for King Saul (**1 Samuel 15**) & and Eli and his sons (**1 Samuel 2**) elapsed. Why is this important? Any individual in sin loses access to spiritual air supply (**Romans 6:1-2**). Such an individual is on borrowed time, based on the remaining air in their lungs. Therefore, the grace period for everyone is different. For example, Both King David and King Saul sinned. However, it was King Saul that was ultimately rejected. Why was that the case? King David always repented before his grace period elapsed, while King Saul never repented.

We see that according to the scriptures, only one thing can make our spiritual air cease. It is disobedience, that is, sin. Sin chokes everything about God out of us. As we know, anything about God within us is a result of God's grace (**1 Corinthians 15:10**). Therefore, when sin chokes this out, we are rendered lifeless spiritually, and spiritual death is the resulting end (**Genesis 3**). Every major sin that can affect our relationship with God is rooted in disobedience to God. Therefore, the only way to remain alive spiritually is to obey God.

As per **John 3:16**, we know that God loves us all. He wants us all to live in abundance (**John 10:10**) spiritually and physically. Hence, He has made provision through Jesus Christ. However, to enjoy God's abundance to the fullest, we must obey Him. Our level of obedience determines our level of grace and the quantity of air available to us spiritually. The grace of God is experienced both physically and spiritually. However, His grace is the air that we breathe spiritually. Without His grace, suffocation from the work of the enemy, that is, spiritual death is inevitable. Therefore, we must intentionally position ourselves to receive fresh spiritual air by obeying God at all times. This will invigorate our spiritual life and spiritual growth.

Food

Food is one of the basic needs of life. Food gives our body the nutrients it needs to stay alive and grow. Food is essential in the physical; likewise, it is also vital in the spiritual. Food remains a necessary factor when a new baby is born, from birth to the end of life. Lack of food will lead to death, both physically and spiritually. Hence, spiritual food is vital to stay alive and grow in God.

WHAT IS SPIRITUAL FOOD?

The answer lies in one of Jesus' statements in **John 6:48 AMP**; He said *I am the Bread of Life [the Living Bread which gives and sustains life].* As per **John 6:55**, Jesus used bread here to symbolize food. The interpretation of Jesus' statement here goes as such: *I am the food of life [the Living food which gives and sustains life].* To stay alive, we need the food of life. Our spiritual food is JESUS.

We consume most foods to assimilate their nutrients. The next logical question would be, how am I supposed to eat Jesus? If you are born again or understand the concept of Christianity, you may think this through communion. If you are new to Christianity, you probably don't know. The eating of Jesus' flesh and drinking His blood, as described in **John 6**, probably seemed like a scene from a vampire movie. You are not alone in this line of thought. It was echoed by the Jews when Jesus taught this concept (**John 6:52**).

In the beginning, the Word already existed. The Word was with God, and the Word was God. He existed at the beginning with God. God created everything through him, and nothing was created except through him. The Word gave life to everything that was created, and his life brought light to everyone. (**John 1:1-4 NLT**)

As per the scripture above, the Word was with God initially. So, let's go back to the beginning as we know it.

In the beginning God created the heavens and the earth. The earth was formless and empty, and darkness covered the deep waters. And the Spirit of God was hovering over the surface of the waters. Then God said, "Let there be light," and there was light. (**Genesis 1:1-3 NLT**)

By now, we know and understand the concept of the Trinity. Our God is triune. He exists in the form of the Father, the Son (Jesus) and the Holy Spirit. Each of these forms is God, and together they are also God. From Genesis, we know that the Father created, and the Spirit of God was hovering. This means that the Father and the Holy Spirit were present at creation. Where was the Son (Jesus)? Even though the Son was not yet born physically, He had been part of God's triune nature. This means He existed before He was born here on earth through the virgin. As per John, the Word was there in the beginning. This Word was what the Father declared when He said *let there be light* in Genesis. John continued by saying that *the Word was with God, and the Word was God.* So, if the Word was God, and both the Father and the Holy Spirit were seen explicitly in the beginning, the Word must be Jesus. He is the only part of the Trinity that was not expressly mentioned in Genesis. So, before Jesus existed physically through the virgin birth, He was the Word. Therefore, the Word is referred to in John and Genesis as Jesus. In this way, every Word of God is God (Jesus) personified (**Psalm 138:2b NKJV** - *For You have magnified Your Word above all Your name*).

Furthermore, John added, "*God created everything through Him, and nothing was created except through Him.*" From this portion of scripture, we see that John referred to the Word as Him. He did so because He had established that the Word was God, Jesus. This verse also reveals that creation was brought to existence through the power of the Word. Therefore, the creative power of God is in the Lord—Jesus. We confirm the concept of Jesus being the Word again when Apostle Paul, while talking about Jesus in **Colossians 1:15-16 NLT**, confirms John's revelation by saying that "*Christ is the visible image of the invisible God. He existed before anything was created and is supreme over all creation, for through him, God created everything in the heavenly realms and on earth. He made the things we can see and the things we can't see— such as thrones, kingdoms, rulers, and authorities in the unseen world. Everything was created through him and for him.*"

Now let us discuss what I had earlier alluded to about communion. The concept of communion was introduced in its current way by Jesus in **Matthew 26:26-28** and **Luke 22:19-20**. First, however, we will use Apostle Paul's explanations in this study, as seen in **1 Corinthians 11:23-26**. Before we proceed, let us go back to **John 6:53-58 NLT**.

So, Jesus said again, "I tell you the truth, unless you eat the flesh of the Son of Man and drink his blood, you cannot have eternal life within you. But anyone who eats my flesh and drinks my blood has eternal life, and I will raise that person at the last day. For my flesh is true food, and my blood is true drink. Anyone who eats my flesh and drinks my blood remains in me, and I in him. I live because of the living Father who sent me; in the same way, anyone who feeds on me will live because of me. I am the true bread that came down from heaven. Anyone who eats this bread will not die as your ancestors did (even though they ate the manna) but will live forever."

In summary, Jesus said that we could not have eternal life (here on earth or after death) unless we ate His flesh and drank His blood. From the scriptures, there are two ways that we follow this prescription of Jesus. The first is communion and the second is through the Word. Now let's dive into each way for better understanding.

THE COMMUNION

For I pass on to you what I received from the Lord himself. On the night when he was betrayed, the Lord Jesus took some bread and gave thanks to God for it. Then he broke it in pieces and said, "This is my body, which is given for you. Do this in remembrance of me." In the same way, he took the cup of wine after supper, saying, "This cup is the new covenant between God and his people—an agreement confirmed with my blood. Do this in remembrance of me as often as you drink it." For every time you eat this bread and drink this cup, you are announcing the Lord's death until he comes again. (1 Corinthians 11:23-26 NLT)

The communion ceremony was a command by our Lord and Savior—Jesus. By fulfilling this command, we are remembering and announcing His death. When we take

Communion, we eat the flesh and drink the blood of Jesus sacrificed on the cross. In this way, Communion does re-enact the works of Jesus on the cross. So, when Communion is done right, as specified in **1 Corinthians 11**, any request and deliverance can be received by faith. This is one of the mysteries of God that only the Spirit of God can explain to us.

Communion is a transaction between God and His Children. The sacrifice of Jesus established this covenant with God. Therefore, when we key into that covenant, we have access to what Jesus made available. When Jesus said, "do this in remembrance of Him," He wasn't worried about being forgotten; He wanted a tradition that brings about the memory of Jesus. This act also brings the past works of Jesus on the cross to the present. Every time we do it, it is as if Jesus just died and made all good things available to us anew. We are reinforcing memories of the devil's failure and the victory of Jesus.

Just as we all have different emotional attachments and reactions to other traditions, so is this in the Spirit. The Spiritual realm stands at attention, just as it did when Jesus originally died over 2,000 years ago. Therefore, miracles, signs and wonders must always happen when Communion is done right in faith. Jesus' work affects all aspects of our being; hence, expect this flow of deliverance in all aspects of our being. Of course, like anything in Christianity, it is not the act, but the faith behind that enables the result. So, when this is appropriately done in faith, mind-blowing results are inevitable. This is not the food for our Spirit to grow. Instead, it is a weapon that continually opens doors for us. For a better understanding, let's use the thanksgiving holiday as a case study. The United States and Canada have foods associated with this tradition. Eating turkey and stuffing is a common practice during thanksgiving. However, the purpose of thanksgiving is not necessarily about eating these foods; it is about being thankful. Likewise, in the communion tradition, we pray to transform the food and drink into the body and the blood of Jesus. Then, we proceed with consuming the food and drink. However, the purpose of Communion is not necessarily about eating food; it is about re-enacting the work of Jesus. So, we generate massive power needed for deliverance and other spiritual affairs. It is essential to state that eating Jesus' flesh is not enough to grow spiritually; the Word of God is needed to grow spiritually.

EATING THE SPIRITUAL FOOD (THE WORD OF GOD)

God is the source and sustenance of our lives (John 1:3). Therefore, to stay alive in God's spirit world, we must eat God-given food. What is the food of the Spirit? Let us answer this question by examining an incident in **Matthew 4**. This was when the devil tempted Jesus with physical food. Jesus had just fasted for forty days and nights and was very hungry.

Then Jesus was led by the Spirit into the wilderness to be tempted there by the devil. For forty days and forty nights he fasted and became very hungry. During that time the devil came and said to him, "If you are the Son of God, tell these stones to become loaves of bread." But Jesus told him, "No! The Scriptures say, 'People do not live by bread alone, but by every word that comes from the mouth of God.'" (**Matthew 4:1-4 NLT**)

From the scripture above, we discover that Jesus overcame by saying humans need more than physical food to live and what is required is every Word that comes out of God's mouth. Hence, the Word of God is food because we need it to live. Yes, bread (physical food) is good for the body, but the Word of God is superior. Why? Because the Word is beneficial to both the Spirit and the body. Therefore, when the Word of God declares a thing under the right circumstances, even our physical body will come into alignment and receive whatever was said. This validates the superiority of the Word of God.

Furthermore, this first temptation was aimed at challenging Jesus' understanding of His identity, hence the word "if you are the Son of God." Jesus replied by saying that His physical state does not define Him. Yes, He was physically hungry at that time. But Jesus is the Word, so He had excellent food. As such, He had no problem physically. Therefore, Jesus said in **John 6:51 NLT**, "*I am the living bread that came down from heaven. Anyone who eats this bread will live forever; and this bread, which I will offer so the world may live, is my flesh.*" When we are filled with the Word, we should have no physical problems. Jesus had no reason to doubt His Sonship because He had the Word of God that affirmed that. There are no issues in life without a Word. The Word is the solution to all matters of life. Anything that can affect us negatively or positively, whether physical or spiritual, requires the Word.

Jesus was not spiritually starving, so He could confront the devil's lies. Jesus countered the devil by quoting the Word He already knew. Just as we solve physical hunger with food, we must oppose any attack against us with the Word. Jesus, being the Word, means He does not lack the Word. The devil never rebutted Jesus' claim about the Word being the food of life; instead, he moved on to tempt Jesus in another way. We must understand that all our physical deficiencies and gaps in our walk with God indicate the deficiency of the Word in our lives. Therefore, the Word of God is imperative to stay strong and have a healthy life, both physically and spiritually.

As noted earlier, there is "the Word" for every situation. The Word that God has given to each person is the food for that person. Hence the Word is personal. You can learn from someone else's prognosis, but you must get your prescription. In that sense, the Word given by God to each person contains what that person needs to stay alive and grow in both realms. Thus, there are different words for different needs.

In the physical, not eating will eventually lead to death. Likewise, failing to feed on the Word will lead to spiritual death. As per the Bible in **Psalm 119:11** NKJV, "*Your Word I have hidden in my heart, That I might not sin against You.*" We know that God hates sin; sin ends our relationship with God. With this in mind, we can further elaborate on what the psalmist said: "*The Word I have hidden in my heart, that I may stay alive in God's spirit world.*" This verse indicates that if we are to stay alive in God, then the Word is a non-negotiable necessity. It is also saying that keeping the Word in our hearts, not just reading but meditating for understanding (**Joshua 1:8**), has the power to keep us from sin. Meditation converts the Word (raw) to revelation (cooked food).

Another crucial point about the Word is as follows. Sin causes death due to disobedience to God; hence, we must know the will of God to obey Him. The will of God can only be found in the Word of God. The understanding of the will of God is the nutrient that we need. However, it is the study of the Word that gives us these nutrients. The essence of God is in His Word. The Bible says, "*He has magnified His Word above all His name*" (**Psalm 138:2 NKJV**). God's Word is His bond. When we know the will of God for our lives at every point in time, life gets easy, and it becomes impossible to die spiritually or an untimely physical death.

In conclusion, the Word is personal. It is your prescription. It is the food meant for you alone. Therefore, the type and quantity of food required depend solely on your growth needs. You cannot determine which food will satisfy your spiritual growth needs. Only God can do that because He created you and knows all the intricacies of your being. Unlike the physical, we cannot afford to go without food at any point in time spiritually. If we do not continually eat, we grant the enemy access to destroy us (**1 Peter 5:8** and **Ephesians 6:12**). Therefore, when you stay away from the Word of God, you are simply running into the arms of the devil. The Word being personal means that it is specific to you. You are supposed to obey completely when the Word is given to you. When you disobey the Word given to you, the devil will exploit that to lead you to sin (death). Therefore, we are advised to continually study the Book of Instruction (the Word) and meditate on it day and night, so we will be sure to obey everything written in it; it is only then we will prosper and succeed in all we do (**Joshua 1:8**, emphasis added). Therefore, always get your Word from God, process it correctly by meditating on it to gain understanding, and live by it.

The Word Avenue

The next logical question is, how do we get this essential food of life? Having read the previous section, many might assume that the only avenue is the Bible. Even though this is true and ultimate, God uses a variety of ways to give us the needed food for life. God can neither be confined nor fathomed. He can provide us with our spiritual food in any way He deems fit. He is the Almighty who is unchanging (**Malachi 3:6**), mightier than all (**Psalm 135:5**), and cannot be boxed in (**Isaiah 55:9**). It is imperative to state that any way that God exploits to give us the food of life will always be in alignment with scriptures. As we have learnt, the Word is food and must be ingested consistently—day and night. Therefore, we must always ask God for our daily food. In teaching the disciples to pray, Jesus incorporated this in **Matthew 6:11 NLT** by saying, *"give us today the food we need."* God has created guaranteed ways for us to always have the Word in His infinite mercy. Due to the sovereign nature of God, it is impossible to discuss all the methods, but we will highlight a few.

The Bible

There is no way to discuss the Word of God in this day and age without the Bible. The Bible is the raw embodiment of the Word of God. When the Word of God is mentioned, many assume that reference is being made to the Bible. This is rightfully so because the Bible is the Word of God. But how is the Bible the Word of God? Did God write the Bible?

The Bible is a collection of scriptures or sacred books. It contains two canons—the old testament and the new testament. The Bible has 66 books in total—39 books in the old testament and 27 in the new testament. The Bible today is one of the world's oldest books. Based on translations, interpretations and the number of copies sold, it is an all-time bestseller. Yes, it is a Christian book, but its principles and content make it relevant and valuable to all. Revelation is the last and most recent book in the Bible, in terms of the date it was written. It was estimated to have been written between 94–96 AD. Per history, the Bible was written by different humans throughout many dispensations. But how is this collection of books the Word of God? And how come only these books were selected for the collection?

2 Timothy 3:16 NLT said, "*all Scripture is inspired by God and is useful to teach us what is true and to make us realize what is wrong in our lives. It corrects us when we are wrong and teaches us to do what is right.*" There are two things to pay attention to from this scripture. First, every book that made its way into the Bible was inspired by God. This means that God inspired the authors, who then wrote these books under the inspiration of God. Does this mean that God did not inspire other books not contained in the Bible? Before I answer this question, we must understand that God is the Almighty and the master planner. *Every Word of God is either a Word of knowledge (information) or a Word of wisdom (solution to problems) for the present time. However, the Word is always a Word of prophecy for the future.* God, who knows the future, strategically filters out the Word that we need today out of the many Words He gave in times past. Yes, each book of the Bible was written at different times but made it into the Bible because of God's ordination. Some authors of these books could not learn how or when the Word will be relevant (**1 Peter 1:10-16**). Hence, if any

book is not in the Bible (the 66 sacred texts), it was either not inspired by God or irrelevant for this dispensation, in accordance with God's wisdom. It will be unwise to read such books for spiritual purposes.

Many might say that the old testament is not relevant today. This statement is both correct and incorrect at the very same time. In **Isaiah 55:8 NLT**, God said, "*My thoughts are nothing like your thoughts, says the LORD. And my ways are far beyond anything you could imagine.*" This means interpreting the Word of God in our literal understanding is not wise. Some words (such as parables, proverbs, and metaphors) may superficially appear irrelevant if interpreted literally. Hence, the Spirit of God is needed to solve problems from a place of depth. Jesus alluded to this in **Matthew 13:11**. This is why reading the Word is not enough; we must always invite the one who inspired the Word to give us insight.

The Bible is not an ordinary book. The majority of what is compiled in it is spiritually redacted. You know the Word is there, but you cannot see it. It is just as though there is a Word behind the Word. Everything we need to know about God in this life is in His Word. The secret of God is in His Word. These secrets are secured in His Word through redactions and encryptions. For example, there were prophecies about the birth, life, death, and resurrection of Jesus Christ. However, the devil was still taken aback (**1 Corinthians 2:8**). He didn't realize that Jesus' work on the cross was salvation for humanity. Even though this secret and mystery of God were out in the open through the prophecies of His prophets, it was encrypted. Therefore, every secret of God that we need to know for our upliftment and relationship with Him is already in His Word. However, only God can decrypt it for us when we seek revelation from His Word.

The devil already knows anything we can decipher with our human understanding. When we receive revelation from God, the devil will remain oblivious to the revelation, unless we ignorantly give it to him. Therefore, *the secret of the LORD is with those who fear Him, And He will show them His covenant.* (**Psalm 25:14 NKJV**). *The LORD our God has secrets known to no one. We are not accountable for them, but we and our children are accountable forever for all that he has revealed to us, so that we may obey all the terms of these instructions.* (**Deuteronomy 29:29 NLT**).

Now let us turn our attention to something interesting. When a Christian preacher preaches, or a teacher teaches, they must always refer to the Bible to back up their assertions. It is as if the integrity of everything in Christianity is validated once it is backed up with Biblical citations. Hence references are cited. But why? As per **Ecclesiastes 1:9 NKJV**, "*that which has been is what will be, that which is done is what will be done, and there is nothing new under the sun.*" Here is the fact, God is not re-creating; we are simply evolving in our understanding. What this means is everything new to us is not new. We are just discovering them.

The Bible was strategically put together by God for us today. Despite many attempts to destroy it, the Bible is still here. Therefore, every revelation we get today must directly, indirectly or figuratively be verified by the Bible. If it is not, I assure you it is not from God. This is because, in **Psalm 89:34 NKJV**, God said *My covenant, I will not break, nor alter the Word that has gone out of My lips.* So, if nothing is new, He has given the Word in the past. If God made that Word available in the Bible today, then any so-called revelation is not new; it is simply a decrypted Word from the scriptures. Therefore, before we agree with any principle, we must be like the Bereans that sought scriptural references (**Acts 17:11**). When we receive a revelation from God, we should ask Him to show it to us from the Bible. It is always there; we need help to see it. Hence, every principle of Christianity must be backed up by the Bible. This makes the Bible the handbook of Christianity. The base of Christendom is the Word of God—the Bible.

Anointed Books

To be anointed is to be under the influence of the Holy Spirit. In the same way, anointed books simply mean books written under the inspiration of the Holy Spirit. Everything written in an anointed book contains information, concepts, and principles by the Holy Spirit. It could be what He has revealed or is still revealing to the writer. In discussing the Bible, we said it is a collection of sacred books written by humans under the Holy Spirit's inspiration. In a way, these sacred books of the Bible are anointed. Therefore, any book written under the inspiration of the Holy Spirit, like this one, is an anointed book. But as we will learn soon, though the Holy Spirit inspired the Bible and books such as this, the Bible remains superior. Every other anointed book must reference the Bible directly; otherwise, it is not anointed.

We have established that there is nothing new under the sun (**Ecclesiastes 1:9**). Therefore, there is no new revelation, but instead, newly discovered revelations. Because it has always existed. In **Proverbs 25:2 NLT**, the Bible made us understand that it is *God's privilege to conceal things* *and the king's privilege to discover them.* As was alluded to earlier, God conceals His secrets not to hide them from us but from the devil. **Psalm 25:14 NKJV** says *the secret of the LORD is with those who fear Him, And He will show them His covenant.* This implies that for God to reveal His mysteries, He must trust us. The more we fear God (that is, to have reverence and respect for Him) and get close to Him, the more He will trust us with more secrets. Therefore, the promises of **Jeremiah 33:3** and **Matthew 7:7** are on solid ground for those that fear God. Everything we will ever need is already in the Bible, but only a genuinely close relationship with God can unlock these revelations. I am writing this anointed book to teach you the secret I have unlocked based on my relationship with God.

    Isaac Newton said, "If I have seen further, it is by standing on the shoulders of giants." Elisha got the double portion of Elijah by studying, understanding, and sticking with him till the end. Without reinventing the wheel, he got double the portion of what Elijah had (**2 Kings 1-2**). When God releases anything here on the earth, it remains here (**Romans 11:29**); it does not return to God. Even though Elisha died with the double portion, the ardor of the power he received did not wane (**2 Kings 13:21**). This is the reason behind the demonic doctrine and practice of grave sucking, which is wrong. Per **1 John 5:14**, our job is to ask God according to His will. He will then take whatever we are asking out of wherever it is (**Isaiah 45:3**). Only God has the absolute right to take anything from anywhere (**Psalm 24:1**). It is demonic to go around hunting for what is not yours. Many people have gone ahead of us in God; they have walked with Him and accumulated His secrets from what He has revealed to them. When such people write, they are doing that from a place of depth and understanding. Such books are anointed because they write about what God has revealed to them. They are decoding and bringing out revelations concealed in the Bible. They have the revelation, and it is here on earth. What might take another five years to discover is now encapsulated in a book. However, once we read these books, we can get the secrets written for our benefit.

Here is another fact, the Bible is timeless, even though it was written at a particular point in time past. Thus, the language and the analogy used in the Bible correspond with the evolution of human understanding at the time it was written. God and His Word have not changed, but humanity is evolving in understanding. This evolution affects everything about us. For instance, what it might take to understand a revelation in the 1800s will differ from the 1900s. Therefore, another purpose of anointed books is to decode a portion or topic of the Bible and adapt it to the understanding of the time. The writer has had the privilege via the Holy Spirit to these secrets in their day and age. Therefore, there are always relevant anointed books on any topic or concept of life at every point.

As Christians, our point of reference is the Bible. Any book today that does not draw from the treasures of the Bible, explain the Bible or bring the Bible to life in this day and age doesn't fall into the category of anointed books. Even when the Holy Spirit speaks or gives insights, He never goes against the Bible; instead, He expounds on the Bible for understanding. Every newly discovered insight from God always references His Word—the Bible. Jesus, Apostle Paul, and Peter all referenced the written Word of God of their time in their writings and teachings. Anointed books are written to explain the Bible or bring it to life in a relatable way. In this way, we can say that anointed books are supplementary materials for Christianity.

Finally, anointed books are God's inspired books. As per Jesus in **Matthew 4:4**, our food of life is every Word of God. Therefore, these books are also the food of life meant for our spiritual life and growth. However, as per **Romans 8:14**, we must be led by the Spirit of God. There are many anointed books, but the Spirit of God must lead us to the right food. This is when it becomes beneficial. It is also imperative to state that although certain foods are not for you, it has nothing to do with their integrity. Unless the Lord tells you that food is bad, you must be careful not to blaspheme the work of the Holy Spirit (**Matthew 12:31**). Remember, one man's food may be another man's allergy. Therefore, leave the food that is not yours and take in the food that is for you.

Anointed Messages

One guaranteed way that God speaks to us today is by sending us "anointed messages," also called "a Word in season." It can come in the form of teaching, preaching or prophecies. Due to the variety of ways these messages can be received, different vessels may be used by God. These vessels used by God are the messengers. As such, anointed messages are inspired by the Holy Spirit with an affirmation from the Bible.

We have established that God is our heavenly Father. Therefore, it is fair to ask, why do we need messengers to give us a message from God? While this is a valid question, there are many reasons for this. All through the Bible, we saw God sending messengers to people to deliver messages.

This is the way of God in providing certain Words. Also, we must understand that every one of us has a blind spot. Therefore, in such areas of our lives, God will use another trusted vessel to ensure we are cognizant of His nudge. For example, even though Moses heard God clearly and spoke with Him face-to-face (**Exodus 33:11**), God still used his father-in-law to deliver the word of wisdom he needed (**Exodus 18**). Furthermore, It is also God's way of keeping us humble because He abhors pride (**Proverbs 8:13**).

Due to this reason, God has placed us in a spiritual family and surrounded us with people so He can speak through them when needed. For this reason, we are advised to *not neglect our meeting together, as some people do, but encourage one another, especially now that the day of his return is drawing near* (**Hebrews 10:25 NLT**). One sure place God created, for this reason, is the church—the body of Christ. Therefore, *Christ gave to the church: the apostles, the prophets, the evangelists, and the pastors and teachers. Their responsibility is to equip God's people to do his work and build up the church, the body of Christ* (**Ephesians 4:11-12 NLT**). These vessels must always be available to ensure the church is fed fresh food. God appoints these people, and He alone can flow through them as He deems fit. Yes, there are qualifications specified for such people as per the scriptures. But is this the only way God speaks within His Church? No! God cannot be boxed in; He alone decides who to talk through. However, these fivefold ministries in the church are the primary communication vessels; every other vessel within a church is secondary.

Unlike some other gods, our God speaks and hears. This avenue brings that alive because God communicates with us in real time. God communicates with us through preaching, teaching or prophecy in real-time. For instance, there are many things that God may want us to do today but might not be found literally in the Bible. For example, suppose God wants a person to move to Atlanta. In that case, it will be impossible to find that literally in the Bible. But God using the fivefold ministries makes it very easy to hear God clearly with the backing of the Bible as it relates to the individual.

Also, the Word in this form is a way for us to learn about God, His ways, and His acts. This is the only way we can get close to Him. In Christianity today, our existence and growth in God are underpinned by our learning from the Word. Prophecy informs us about the mind of God, and preaching tells us about our capacity. In contrast, teaching informs us how to get things done. These are all forms of learning. To grow in life, learning is not an option but a necessity. Therefore, learning is an essential need in life. Someone said, "the day you stop learning, you start dying." Though this is primarily true, the quality of what we learn determines our growth or untimely death. For instance, even though food is essential to stay alive, some foods can propagate untimely death.

Based on what we've discussed, we know that the Word is the essential food. Therefore, prophecies, preachings, and teachings based on the Word are not an option in Christianity but a necessity. Just like the concept of anointed books, anointed prophecies, anointed preachings, and anointed teachings are also inspired by the Holy Spirit and based on the Bible.

God uses anointed messages to relate the Word to our present. Therefore, every time God speaks through this medium, His goal is to give us understanding. Though the

Bible is ancient, and some of its contents might not appear relatable in the present day, our God is a specialist in making the un-relatable relatable. Therefore, we must be cautious of any message that does not reference the Bible or bring about the understanding of God if we want to grow spiritually.

Anointed messages are sources of spiritual food because they emanate from the Holy Spirit. Ideally, we learn from those ahead of us. The Spirit of God is way ahead of us in understanding, and we can learn from Him. Educational institutions must have teachers, lecturers, and professors to aid learning. Likewise, in the spiritual, a healthy Church must have spiritual vessels (the fivefold ministries) that God has chosen for His assignments to help our learning and growth.

Inner Witness of The Holy Spirit

One thing that distinguishes us as children of God is the Holy Spirit. He is the Spirit of God promised to every child of God (**John 14:16**). Therefore, He is only meant for the Children of God. *The world cannot receive Him because it isn't looking for Him and doesn't recognize Him. But you know Him because He lives with you now and later will be in you* (**John 14:17** NLT).

In **John 14:6** NLT, Jesus said, "*I am the way, the truth, and the life. No one can come to the Father except through me.*" The primary goal is the Father, who is the creator of all. Our relationship with Him was severed when Adam and Eve sinned at the beginning (**Genesis 3**). However, the Father, in His mercy, saw humanity's struggle with the devil and reconciled us back to Himself through Jesus Christ (2

Corinthians 5:18). Therefore, Jesus is the door to the Father (John 10:9). However, between the door and the Father are steps leading to purity and perfection. As per **Habakkuk 1:13 NLT**, *"God is pure and cannot stand the sight of evil."* Hence, to approach the Father, we must also be pure. This is the essence of the steps between the door and the Father. Like the thief on the cross in **Luke 23:42-43**, those who die immediately after receiving salvation skip these steps of purity and perfection. Notwithstanding, so long as you are still alive on earth after receiving salvation, you must walk these steps leading to purity and perfection.

The moment we become saved, we are hidden in Jesus Christ. God sees us in light of Jesus, who is already pure and perfect (**Colossians 3:3**). We must remain hidden in Christ, so we approach our heavenly Father unblemished (**Ephesians 5:27**). We are to be perfect, even as our Father in heaven is perfect (**Matthew 5:48 NLT**). However, there is a significant distance between *"where we gave our life to Jesus"* and *"where we become perfect like God."* Therefore, the moment we enter through Jesus—the door, there is a Helper who will guide us through the process of becoming holy, pure, and perfect. This Helper is the Holy Spirit (**John 14:26**). But in the meantime, as we are being perfected, Jesus will shield us and give us access to the Father and present us as holy, pure and perfect. Jesus' credibility in purity and perfection helps us to approach the Father (**2 Corinthians 5:21**), while the Holy Spirit perfects us. Thus, we must always come to the Father in the name of Jesus (**John 14:13**). There is no other way!

The Holy Spirit connects with our spirit and communicates with us from there (**Romans 8:16**). He is the inner witness. He leads, trains and guides us daily as we walk toward purity and perfection. He is our purity and perfection trainer; He works with us here on earth to ensure we are pure and perfect when we meet the Father face-to-face in heaven. This is because *nothing evil will be allowed to enter (Heaven), nor anyone who practices shameful idolatry and dishonesty* (**Revelations 21:27 NLT**).

The Holy Spirit is the Spirit of God. As such, He knows God's mind and will. **1 Corinthians 2:11 NLT** tells us, "*we know that no one can know a person's thoughts except that person's own Spirit, and no one can know God's thoughts except God's own Spirit.*" The Holy Spirit knows what is holy, pure and perfect from God's point of view. So, He aligns us with God's mind by informing and advising us. The Holy Spirit's connection with our spirit makes it easy for Him to know our thoughts (**Proverbs 20:27**). Based on what He sees in our inner being, He advises, corrects and realigns us to God's perfection as much as possible. Of course, since God does not impose Himself on us, the work of the Holy Spirit will only yield the right results when we obey.

This medium of getting fed is one of the most effective and guaranteed ways today. As Christians, we must understand that once we give our lives to Jesus, establishing a connection with the Holy Spirit is the next urgent thing. For some people, it happens immediately, while for others, it happens subsequently. Regardless of the timeframe of the connection, we must ensure we have the inner witness of the Holy Spirit before we move on. The Apostles were not allowed to proceed after the death of Jesus until they established this connection (**Luke 24:49**). I cannot stop emphasizing that this is the essential thing that must be done right after salvation. Without establishing a relationship with the Holy Spirit, we will starve as Children of God. He is so vital that without Him, the Bible becomes a regular book that is very tedious to read. The Holy Spirit is our seal after salvation; therefore, we can lose our salvation without Him (**Ephesians 4:30**). Christianity is very difficult/impossible without the Holy Spirit. Everything the Holy Spirit tells us will directly or indirectly align with the Bible. As such, His job is to give us insight and explain the Bible. In so doing, He reveals to us the heart of our heavenly Father. For more understanding of the Holy Spirit, please read the book I authored, "The Most Important Person of Our Time.

Spiritual Authorities and Servants of God

The servants of God and spiritual authority are another way God speaks to His children and feeds them. These two are similar in that they are God-ordained, though there are nuances. As we will see, having these two in one chosen vessel of God is possible.

As the name implies, a servant of God is a person God has ordained and appointed to use. Such a person proceeds to relinquish their life to God for Him to use as He deems fit (**Romans 1:1**). Remember, God is neither a taskmaster nor a slavemaster. He will not impose Himself on anyone. It remains the prerogative of any individual to intentionally and willingly give themselves to God as a servant. Being a servant of God entails being sold out to God and willing to be used as He wishes. Being a servant means that God is your master, and He dictates every area of your life. An example of such was Prophet Hosea. God asked him to marry a prostitute so that He could communicate a message to the people of that time and people in these times (**Hosea 1 and 3**).

Spiritual Authority, on the other hand, is slightly different. Yes, they can be a servant of God as well. But they are the individuals God has chosen as the delegated authority over a person. In other words, they are God's proxy here on earth over a person. Hence, they are responsible for the well-being of the individual God has appointed them over. For example, Elisha called Elijah his father, even though they were not blood relations (**2 Kings 2:12**); likewise, King Jehoash called Elisha his father (**2 Kings 13:14**). The principle of spiritual authority is at work in both examples. Spiritual authority is a person God has chosen to parent an individual.

Therefore, *children are a gift from the LORD; they are a reward from him* (**Psalm 127:3** NLT). The fact is that we are all God's children, and parenting is a delegated role. As such, God chooses the individuals and entrusts them with responsibilities. Our earthly biological parents and spiritual parents are both forms of delegated authority from God; it is God that chose them. Generally, a child of God will have an earthly biological and spiritual parent. Typically, the birth parent is the authority in physical things, while the spiritual parent is the authority in spiritual things. However, because the spiritual is superior to the physical, the God-ordained spiritual parent can be responsible for the entirety of a believer's life.

Since spiritual authority is a delegated role from God to humans, it is apparent that God is the ultimate spiritual authority. Therefore, if God is the one that chooses these people, then He can very well speak through any one of them and give us our spiritual food through them. Many are conversant with servants of God and spiritual authorities and can relate to them. However, some struggle to believe

God can speak through unbelieving biological parents. You must understand that even though they are unbelievers and unclean vessels, God can temporarily use them. When anything pertains to a child of God, God will exploit any possible avenue to speak to or direct them. For example, David's father (Jesse) sent him on an errand leading to his triumph and glory. Jesse had no idea that God was using him to push David to the top (**1 Samuel 17**). Through David's obedience to his father's instruction, He was positioned to realize his destiny of victory. Generally, we must strive always to remain sensitive to God; in so doing, we will know when God is speaking to us through any means.

Fellow Believers

The earth is human's domain (**Genesis 1:28**). Therefore, a human is needed for God or the devil to bring their plans to fruition on the earth. Every human on the face of the earth is an available vessel for God's or the devil's use. It is always evident who has been yielded to by the actions taken and fruits produced (**Matthew 7:16**).

A believer is an individual that has been saved by God through Jesus and has yielded to the leading of the Spirit of God (**Romans 8:14**). By this definition, a believer is a vessel available to God. This implies that God can use such a person anytime, so long as they are in tune with Him. Our interactions with fellow believers can give us the food that we need. Therefore, *as iron sharpens iron, so a friend sharpens a friend.* (**Proverbs 27:17 NLT**).

We must also understand that everybody has a past, present, and aspirations. This is what makes us who we are. There is no need to reinvent the wheel when a fellow believer has experienced something. We can get the information from them and skip many steps. I had an interesting experience with God that put this into perspective. There was a piece of information the Lord wanted to share with me. But there was another critical information I needed beforehand for what God planned to share with me to make sense. God guided my steps, and I found myself in a conversation with a fellow believer. He shared a few things he had learned from God in our discussions. It made little impact at the time, but the floodgates opened when I got into my quiet time with God. In hindsight, the heavens would have remained shut without that information from a fellow believer. Therefore, if specific information is already within your reach, God may direct you to it rather than share it with you. Moses and Jethro are very relevant examples here again (**Exodus 18**).

We might be wondering why God works like this. Well, it is God's way of keeping us in fellowship with each other and humility. The fact is, to work with God, we must be humble. As my spiritual Father has said, "in God, the way up is down." *God opposes the proud but gives grace to the humble.* (**James 4:6, NLT**). If we are of God and are led by God, all our steps will be in humility. So, God giving us our food this way is an excellent way to humble us. We may not know it all, but God does.

"We have become humble when we know that God uses us as well as others; and when we understand that God equally loves us and others." [Emmanuel Adewusi]. Do not look down on another believer just because of their current status; you must understand that every one of us is a product of God's grace with an unfathomable future (**1 Corinthians 2:9**).

Water

In the daily life of any human, water is a top necessity. It is a critical element for human existence; it is impossible to survive without it. For instance, one of the reasons that the search for another habitable planet has remained tedious is the inability to locate water. According to science, the earth is the only known planet in which water is ubiquitous. Some other discovered and verified planets have fallen short of having the required elements for human survival. For those following recent developments about space, you will know that one of the measures proposed to make Mars habitable is creating a system to supply water to the colony constantly. Any human habitation without sufficient water will experience undue hardship. The City of Flint, Michigan, is yet to recover from its water crisis of 2014 fully. Needless to say, the absence of water is simply the end of life.

In the same way, water is essential to our spirituality. To remain alive after receiving salvation, we must drink water. Of course, the equivalent of water in the spiritual realm is different from the physical realm. However, its necessity and criticality for our spiritual life here on earth are very similar. Without spiritual water, spiritual death is inevitable.

As we have established earlier, there is nothing new under the sun. We will uncover our spiritual water with a few scriptures.

Let us start our studies from Jesus' statement in **John 7:38-39 NLT.**

Anyone who believes in me may come and drink! For the Scriptures declare, 'Rivers of living water will flow from his heart.'" (When he said "living water," he was speaking of the Spirit, who would be given to everyone believing in him. But the Spirit had not yet been given, because Jesus had not yet entered into his glory.)

The scripture above shows that the Bible explicitly explains what water is. From this verse, we see that water is Spirit. Hence, the living water is the Holy Spirit, while dead water is demonic spirits. Therefore, the Holy Spirit is the water we need to stay alive in God while here on earth. Without Him, it is impossible to exist in God's Spiritual World. This was why Jesus told his disciples to stay in the city until the Holy Spirit came and filled them with power from heaven (**Luke 24:49 NLT**). He said this to communicate its importance by letting us know that we cannot survive without the Holy Spirit. Hence, when the Holy Spirit does not support the salvation of an individual, retrogression is inevitable (**2 Corinthians 1:22**). The Bible tells us that "*all who the Spirit of God leads are children of God*" (**Romans 8:14 NLT**). Therefore, if the Spirit of God is not leading you, you are dead to God. In the same way, there is no life where there is no water. Hence, without the Holy Spirit, there is no life in God.

As we have explained earlier, God gave us water to sustain life in the physical realm. However, to stay alive in God's spiritual world, we need God to sustain us (**Psalm 54:4**). Hence, God is our spiritual water. Even though we are still alive, Jesus is no longer physically present here. He returned to heaven and is currently seated at the Father's right hand (**Mark 16:19**). However, He promised us the Holy Spirit (**John 14:16-17**). The Holy Spirit is our water and our indispensable resource on the earth today. For more understanding, I encourage you to read the book I authored, "The Most Important Person of Our Time.

Furthermore, from **Isaiah 12:2-3** NKJV, the scripture establishes that God is our salvation.

Behold, God is my salvation, I will trust and not be afraid; 'For YAH, the LORD, is my strength and song; He also has become my salvation.'" Therefore, with joy you will draw water from the wells of salvation.

This is true today because God, through Jesus, has become our salvation (**2 Timothy 1:9**). Therefore, the latter part of the above scripture says: *It is with joy that we can draw water from the wells of God.* The scripture also specified that there are several wells. Hence, there are many things available to us in these wells. But it is only through the joy which comes with salvation (**Psalm 51:12**) that we can draw from these wells. It is evident that when a person comes to Christ, one of the first things they experience is joy. This is the joy that gives access to the wells of salvation. So, it is only through salvation that we can access these wells of salvation's content (water). We know that we run into different issues that need our attention in life. For every issue we encounter, the solution is contained in these wells. There are many other wells out there, but the content of the wells of salvation distinguishes it. From the scriptures, we see that through Jesus, there is one divine access that cannot be duplicated or found anywhere else. He is the Holy Spirit and is only available through Jesus (**John 14:17**). Could He be the water from the wells of salvation? Indeed, He is. For example, if you are willing to drink from the well of healing, there are many counterfeit healing wells out there. The only healing from God is the healing well of salvation, which comes through Jesus. In this well is the content called the Holy Spirit; His power brings about healing. However, access only comes through the joy that comes from Jesus.

Also, we know from **Galatians** 5:22 that joy, the requirement for the wells, is the fruit of the Holy Spirit. Using the logic of agriculture, you get an orange tree when you plant a seed from an orange fruit. In the same way, when we launch the fruit of the Holy Spirit—joy—into the wells of salvation, the Holy Spirit is what we get. These wells contain the answers to all life issues, but it is only through joy that we can access these answers. Therefore, when we approach the wells with joy, the Holy Spirit responds from the particular well we are inquiring about. This makes Him the water we are drawing from the wells of salvation. When we interpret this scripture based on the explanation, it becomes: Therefore, with the fruit of the Holy Spirit, the Holy Spirit shall respond out of the wells of God.

Look After Yourself

Continuing with our physical metaphor, what does it mean to look after ourselves? In the physical, we know that this is crucial if we want to live long. To look after ourselves implies that we have to take time to study our bodies. We truly understand what is beneficial and damaging to our bodies. We are well aware of what is going on with our bodies. Due to this awareness, our food intake and activities are dictated by what is beneficial to our bodies. When we know a thing like how many calories we need, this is an indication that we know our body. The fact is that we cannot stay healthy physically without knowing our bodies.

So far, everything we have discussed in this chapter is about looking after ourselves in the Spirit. Home, air, food, and water are all required in the correct quantity for healthy living.

However, there is a critical aspect of living healthy that I would like to zoom into. It is taking care of injuries and infirmities. To stay healthy physically, we must take care of injuries. The failure of an individual to take care of injuries can consequently result in their being incapacitated or losing their life. This is also applicable in the spiritual realm.

In the physical, injuries occur due to negligence or accidents. It could have been avoided if injuries had occurred due to negligence. However, we may not have control over injuries that occur due to accidents. It is imperative to state that the severity of injuries will differ; hence, commensurate attention must be given. Whatever the case, we must take good care of any injury to avoid deterioration. It is safe to say that injuries may be inevitable from the nature of injuries and how they may happen.

Now, what is the equivalence of injuries in the spiritual? Looking at the definition of injury in the physical, we can deduce its correspondence in God's spiritual world. A straightforward explanation of injury is simply anything that causes damage to an individual. Injury can be physical or mental. It is anything that causes a person to lose life slowly. For example, a body injury could lead to loss of blood. From the scriptures, we know that there is life in the blood (**Leviticus 17:11**). On the other hand, when injuries are sustained mentally, they can deteriorate to a point where the individual loses their mind or interest in life. Therefore, anything capable of causing the sudden or gradual loss of life is an injury. Using this definition, we can see that spiritual injury and infirmity is sin.

Sin, which means to disobey God, is capable of draining out one's life in God's spiritual world. If it is not well-taken care of, one can lose spiritual air and die (**Romans 6:1**). We need to understand that spiritual injury may be inevitable when a spiritual accident occurs. This does not excuse sin because if we look through the scriptures, we will see that God never condoned sin. However, due to the human nature of imperfections, an accident may occur, and as such, sin happens. When this happens, our focus should be to care for ourselves rather than beat ourselves up.

In some cases, It is usually in hindsight that we realize that we messed up. But, if we do, that is an injury from our silliness. For cases in which the sin resulted from negligence, this is what the Bible admonishes us about in **Romans 6:1**.

In the physical, we know that some people might be more resilient than others. But no one knows how many injuries due to negligence they can sustain before they kill themselves. In the same way, there is a grace level that God may allow an individual to have with such negligence. But the uncanny truth is that we do not know the threshold. For example, David's sin can be deemed negligent and more grievous than Saul's, but David ended up in a better place with God than King Saul. If we continue in negligence, we may lose our spiritual life—salvation.

There is some doctrine going around that I would like to address. As per the Bible, there is no such thing as once saved, forever saved. This purported claim is based on the fact that we are under grace. This is far from the truth because **Romans 6:15 NLT** (*Well then, since God's grace has set us free from the law, does that mean we can go on sinning? Of course not!*) tells us that grace does not excuse sin.

As earlier stated, sin is an injury and must not be permitted if we want to enjoy life. Some may object to what has been said by using the latter part of **Romans 5:20 NLT** (*The law came in so that the trespass would increase; but where sin increased, grace increased all the more*). This may seem logical, but it is a gross misinterpretation of the scripture. From **Romans 6:1**, which comes after **Romans 5:20**, we know that was not what Apostle Paul meant. He was saying that since the devil has increased the capacity of sinners to sin, God has increased His grace coverage for sin if one repents. In that sense, anyone can do nothing beyond God's forgiveness. As my Spiritual Father says, "If Adolf Hitler repented and accepted Jesus while he was here on earth, God would have forgiven him." The moment we accept Jesus, we are redeemed from sin, and the grace coverage no longer applies. The grace coverage is for those in the land of sin. This coverage is unnecessary for those in God's land because sin does not thrive there. Those in God's land are entitled to a different kind of grace.

Genuine Christians sin accidentally and not intentionally. Hence, God has apportioned grace for their adequate coverage (**1 John 1:9**). Because of the nature of a Christian's sin, God allows the Holy Spirit to enable conviction (**John 16:8**). It is the Holy Spirit that lets us know when we sin. He does this before an injury surfaces. Using this logic, we can see that the theory is correct. If we know we have sinned and it is not a mistake, then we don't need anyone to tell us. We must understand that the Holy Spirit is our first responder. He is there to assess the situation and respond appropriately so that the injury is adequately cared for. He is also our doctor when needed. He prescribes and describes the remedy that we need. As the first responder and our doctor, He is trained to give us hope even in dire situations. He is here to convict us (**John 16:8**) and not condemn us. The devil condemns by feeding a person with false information about their condition (**John 8:44**).

So, no matter the gravity of our injury, we must rely on the Holy Spirit to examine it and prescribe solutions accordingly. Do not self-medicate. It is perilous even in the physical realm. Similarly, please do not take another person's prescription; it is equally dangerous. Remember, injuries are serious, no matter how small they are. Leaving it unattended is a highway to a quick and painful death. Whether mental, emotional or spiritual, once you are aware of a possible injury (conviction), consult your doctor—the Holy Spirit. Do not ignore convictions for any reason. They are indications of possible injuries.

Rest

We have heard these words many times. Often it is a prescription for some medical issues. In the physical, when we do not rest, we get to a point where our body refuses to function as it should. This is because everything we do requires the exertion of energy, and rest is a way our body recovers from dissipated energy. We see the importance of rest in labor laws around the world. After a few hours of work, it is required by law to rest. The world has been designed to have a portion of the 24-hour day dedicated to resting. One way of rest that we will be examining here is sleep. It is a mystery how refreshed we feel after a good night's rest—sleep. Sleeping is so crucial that science suggests that one-third of our day is an ideal time for it.

Therefore, knowing what sleep is and doing it in the spiritual realm will make our walk easy.

As usual, to pinpoint what resting is in God's spirit world, we must understand what it is in the physical and equate that to the spiritual. In the physical, when we are asleep, we lose consciousness of our surroundings. There are different stages of sleep; however, science postulates that relaxation comes when we get into a deep sleep. Some people who do not get this kind of sleep may wake up after extended hours and still feel tired. We can see that losing touch physically via deep sleep is essential for good health. Being in a deep sleep is almost similar to being dead. The difference lies in the ability to wake up after being well-rested. The point here is that the equivalence of rest in the spiritual realm entails letting go of things altogether.

The truth from the scriptures is that believers have entered into God's rest (**Hebrews 4:3**). **Hebrews 4:10** gives us an indication of what God's rest means for a believer. However, faith is needed to be a believer (**Romans 10:10**). Hence, faith is also required to enter into God's rest. The moment we enter God's rest, our works or labor ceases. We are not in God's rest on any issue we are still struggling with. How do we rest in God?

Rest in God means to relinquish a situation to the arms of the Father (**1 Peter 5:7**). There was a time when God took on the responsibility of putting us to rest, just as He did for Adam (**Genesis 2:21**). However, this backfired when Adam blamed God for giving Eve to him as a wife (**Genesis 3:12**). Subsequently, it became our responsibility primarily to enter God's rest through Jesus. We now have to strive to enter God's rest (**Matthew 7:7**). One primary way we enter God's rest is through prayer. As I have mentioned, rest means handing a situation's baton to God. At the same time, we watch Him act (**Exodus 14:14**). The only thing we have to do is to approach God through Jesus (**John 14:13**) in faith (**James 1:6**), and we are in God's rest. Then, God takes charge of the situation. This is why the Bible commands us never to *stop praying* (**1 Thessalonians 5:17 NLT**).

It is imperative to understand that entering God's rest does not absolve us of our responsibilities. Refusing to do what we ought to do is a sin (**James 4:17**). God does not condone laziness (**2 Thessalonians 3:10**). God will do His part, and we must do our part. Therefore, we must be able to distinguish our responsibility from God's responsibility. If there is any uncertainty, we can take it to God in prayer, so long as we are sincere and diligent, He will let us know.

To ensure clarity, let's delve deeper here. The essence of rest is for us to have a good and healthy life; it is not for us to be useless. This is why God's movement and every obtainable virtue in Christ require our faith. Faith (**Hebrews 11:6**) and obedience to instructions (**John 14:15**) are our responsibilities. We must understand that even though we are in God's rest, we still have responsibilities. When we are in God's rest, we relinquish the power to get things done to God. However, when He gives us instructions to do something in our realm, we must proceed accordingly. For example, let's say we want a blessing.

Consequently, we prayed and entered into God's rest on that matter. While resting, God may instruct us to do something so that He can bring forth the blessing. In this case, we must act according to God's instruction; God will never take that action on our behalf. Once we've done it in accordance with God's instruction, we continue in His rest while waiting for the manifestation of the blessing.

So, our rest is to relinquish situations to God through the prayer of faith. Once we have the assurance that our prayer is answered, we have entered into His rest. Getting assurance after prayer is critical. It is evident that you have received, even though the manifestation may not yet be physical. Hence, until we have the assurance that our prayer is answered, we are not really in God's rest. As per **John 16:24**, we know we have received the moment our joy is full. Therefore, we enter into God's rest when we experience abundant joy.

Chapter 4

The Growth Process

The Spiritual realm is quite similar to the physical realm. Just as physical growth is essential for a healthy human life, spiritual growth is necessary for a healthy Christian life.

From zygote to newborn, growth is constant. Even after birth, growth is expected in all stages of life. When we do not see the expected growth at the required stage, it could be a problem. Hence, in an ideal state, there is no stagnation. On the other hand, what seemed like stagnation is an indication of a problem. In some cases, a sluggish movement may be interpreted as stagnation. In the same way, there is no stagnation in the spiritual.

2 Chronicles 2:6 helps us to understand the enormity of God. The highest heavens cannot contain Him. If the highest heavens are too small for the King of kings, how much more is the earth? No matter how deep or high we go in our spiritual growth, we can never outgrow the greater One. This is good news! Because God is so big, there is an unimaginable amount of room for us to grow in Him. As children of God, we must strive to grow deeper and higher in the Lord so long as we have air in our lungs.

After many jaw-dropping and life-changing experiences that Paul had, he was still hungry for more of God! His hunger and zeal to draw close to the Lord filled his heart with the words, *"I want to know Christ and experience the mighty power that raised him from the dead"* (**Philippians 3:10 NLT**). Paul discovered that the more he learned about God, the more he realized he did not know. He understood that what he knew and experienced in God was superficial in relation to the unfathomable depths available in God. Beloved, the growth you can experience in God is limitless; Proverbs **4:18 NLT** says that *"the way of the righteous is like the first gleam of dawn, which shines ever brighter until the full light of day."* This scripture affirms that you can grow daily in your walk with Christ, and your relationship with Him can keep getting better. You will never have a better yesterday when you consistently grow in the Lord (**Haggai 2:9**).

Revelations 3:16 NLT (*But since you are like lukewarm water, neither hot nor cold, I will spit you out of my mouth*) elucidates that it is dangerous not to grow in God's spiritual world. Jesus said in **Matthew 7:19 NLT** that *every tree that does not produce good fruit is chopped down and thrown into the fire.* A tree becomes mature when it starts producing fruit. However, it must stay nourished to remain productive; if not, it will be cut down.

As you commence or continue your growth journey, it is essential to know that your development curriculum is solely determined by the Teacher—the Holy Spirit. The things specified in this book are valuable—they are vital for sustaining life and drivers for continuous growth. Doing them enables the development of a reliable foundation on which the Holy Spirit can build. The steps I have provided here can be used as a guide to gauge key areas in your life where growth must continuously be experienced.

Spiritual Exercises

Staying healthy, resting, exercising, and eating well are all essential for healthy physical growth. The more we maintain regular physical exercise, the stronger we become in our physical capacity. This is also valid in the spiritual. When we nourish ourselves with the word of God, anointed worship, anointed messages, and fellowship, we become stronger in our spiritual capacity.

When it comes to exercise, various parts of the body are strengthened. Moreover, physical exercise has many benefits; we look better, healthier and more robust. The interesting thing about exercise is that when we focus on improving a specific body part, we see significant improvement in that area. However, when we balance how we exercise by spending an equal amount of time working on different body parts, we will see that the body will become more physically fit. Exercise that involves and benefits the entire body can be likened to the spiritual activities discussed here.

Just like physical exercise, many spiritual activities can be undertaken; however, we will only discuss some essentials. These essentials are the foundation we can build on with the help of the Holy Spirit.

FELLOWSHIP

Fellowship is to spend quality time with another—engaging in conversations or activities. Fellowship can be done with God or with another human being. At the core of fellowship is quality time. In the same way, time must be invested to see the results of physical exercise and to experience growth in our relationship with God or humans. Only God exists outside of time; we are confined within time. Therefore, our time is our life. Our age, experiences, and achievements result from our invested time. Where we are today is a result of the time we have spent well or wasted. Likewise, our current level of spiritual growth results from the time we have spent well or wasted.

The activities we engage in while fellowshipping are critical. How we use this time can lead to gaining or losing access to a person. Fellowship can be done through conversation, asking questions or engaging in activities that aid person-to-person bonding. When time is wasted, growth is affected.

Another major factor in getting the best out of fellowship is trust. For example, **Psalm 25:14 NKJV** says *the secret of the LORD is with those who fear Him, And He will show them His covenant.* God entrusts His secrets to those who fear Him. He will only share His secrets with those He can trust. Hence, to have genuine and beneficial fellowship with God, we must fear Him—that is, absolute respect, honor, and reverence for Him. In the same way, proper fellowship with humans is only beneficial when we have complete respect and reverence for the other person.

When fellowship is done correctly, we have unhindered access to the treasures given to us by another person. Often these treasures are what we need for growth. Fellowship entails give and take between both parties—virtues are taken from us and added to us. Hence, fellowship is a guaranteed way to experience constant growth. For this reason, fellowship is key to spiritual growth. The more time we spend doing the right thing, the better for us.

Fellowship with God

Earlier, we affirmed that fellowship gives us unhindered access to other people's treasures. In that sense, we can only imagine how many treasures we have access to by fellowshipping with God. So how do we fellowship with GOD?

It may seem impossible, but God, in His mercy, has made it simple and possible. To start us off, let us examine **2 Corinthians 2:11 NLT**. The Bible says *no one can know a person's thoughts except that person's own spirit, and no one can know God's thoughts except God's own Spirit.* This means no one can see another person thoroughly except the spirit of that person. In other words, the depth of a person is attainable through their spirit.

In the same way, we cannot know God without the Spirit of God. In **1 Corinthians 2:10 NLT**, we see that *it was to us that God revealed these things by his Spirit. For His Spirit searches out everything and shows us God's deep secrets.* Therefore, if we are to have access to God's treasures and mysteries, then the Spirit of God is our way in.

We can only fellowship with God on a spirit-to-spirit level. This is why we are commanded to *"worship in spirit and in truth"* in **John 4:24 NLT**. We worship in truth because God only opens up to those He can trust (**Psalm 25:4**). We can fellowship with God in many ways. Whenever we engage the Spirit of God, we are fellowshipping. Worship and prayer are also forms of fellowship. This is why *people who aren't spiritual can't receive these truths from God's Spirit. It all sounds foolish to them, and they can't understand it, for only those who are spiritual can understand what the Spirit means.* (1 Corinthians 2:14 NLT).

From 2 Corinthians 2:11, we see that there is a person's spirit. This is because we are spiritual beings living in a body with a soul. Our spirit makes it easy for us to connect with God through the Spirit of God. As per Romans 8:16 NLT, God's Spirit *joins with our spirit to affirm that we are God's children.* The Spirit of God has access to the treasures in our hearts and God's treasures. The act of fellowship merges these treasures together for our benefit. Without fellowship, we have no access. Therefore, we must spend quality time fellowshipping with God through His Spirit.

For the sake of our studies, we will examine one fellowship enhancer and three methods of fellowship with God. This is not an exhaustive list; it is the basics we can build on with the help of the Holy Spirit.

Method One: Worship

There are many ways to fellowship with God. As per John 4:24, one of these ways is worship. Worship is anything we do out of absolute respect, honor and reverence for God. It is whatever God can interpret as a reflection of our love for Him. The intent of worship is not for us to receive anything from God; it is simply the expression of our love for Him. When worship is done correctly, God grants us unrestricted access to His treasures. For example, Solomon worshipped God with a thousand burnt offerings (2 Chronicles 1:6), and God gave him a blank cheque. Such an offering must have required a lot of resources, energy, and, most importantly, time; hence, it qualifies as a fellowship. God, in turn, came to Him and said, "Here is My treasure; what do you want?" (**2 Chronicles 1:7**).

According to **John 4:24**, two recipes must be included in our worship to count as acceptable. The first is that it must be offered in spirit. The Holy Spirit assists in this regard. The second is that it must be done in truth, which means doing so sincerely. When we do this, God will then, in turn, give us access to His treasures through the Holy Spirit because *anyone who trusts in him will never be disgraced* (**Romans 10:11 NKJV**). We see that to worship; we need the Holy Spirit. He must be our guide and director. He helps us to worship in spirit as well as in truth. Otherwise, even with good intentions, we can bring strange fire before God (**Leviticus 10:1**). A classic example is found in **Acts 5:1-10**. Ananias and Sapphira meant to worship God with their resources. However, they failed to consult the Holy Spirit. They worshiped insincerely in their heart and, in so doing, got destroyed instead of gaining access to God's treasures. It is better not to worship God than to do so outside the parameters outlined. Therefore, without the Spirit of God, true worship is simply impossible.

Method Two: The Word of God

In **Ecclesiastes 1:9 NLT**, the Bible made us understand that *nothing under the sun is truly new.* Everything we need to know about God here on earth has already been released. Therefore, the Bible is the most important book on the face of the earth. This is why God told us in **Joshua 1:8 NLT**, "*Study this Book of Instruction continually. Meditate on it* *day and night so you will be sure to obey everything written in it. Only then will you prosper and succeed in all you do."* This is because, in the Bible, there are treasures for prosperity and success.

When we take time to study and meditate on the Word of God, we connect with God. As we read His Word, we connect with Him. This also qualifies reading the Word as fellowship. We are learning about God, and He is communicating with us from His Word. The Bible is filled with encrypted words meant to unveil treasures if we sincerely connect with God through the Word.

Our hearts must be positioned correctly to experience the full benefit of fellowshipping with God through His Word. Due to the secure nature of the treasure of the Word, we need a guarantor, a person who can vouch for us. The guarantor is the Holy Spirit. He must affirm that we are God's children (**Romans 8:16**) and that we can be entrusted with X. Otherwise, the Word will be another regular book to us. Benefitting from the Word of God without the Holy Spirit is impossible.

Method Three: Prayer

The Last thing we will discuss here is prayer. Prayer is communication with God. Just as there are different kinds of communication, there are different kinds of prayers. One important thing to note here is that prayer can be in any form. Therefore, it involves two people, at the very least. The mechanics of conversation are also the mechanics of prayer. For example, when conversing with someone and you ask them a question, you can expect a response. Similarly, when you are communicating with God in prayer and ask Him a question, you can expect a response. However, we must understand the kind of conversation we are having with God and set our expectations accordingly.

Prayer requires quality time; the time we spend is really up to us. Two things qualify a prayer as fellowship. The first is that it must be done using the name of Jesus. Jesus said in **John 15:16b NLT** that *the Father will give you whatever you ask for, using my name.* This is because Jesus redeemed us (**Galatians 3:13**) and gave us access to the inaccessible (**Ephesians 2:18**). Therefore, we must approach God in Jesus' name. Otherwise, we will not be recognized. The second is that it must also be done with the help of the Holy Spirit. As per **Romans 8:16**, the Holy Spirit connects us with God. We can see that we cannot access God or His treasures without the Spirit of God. His involvement in prayer was spelled out in **Romans 8:26 NLT**, "*And the Holy Spirit helps us in our weakness. For example, we don't know what God wants us to pray for. But the Holy Spirit prays for us with groanings that cannot be expressed in words.*" Therefore, any prayer without Jesus' name and the Holy Spirit is not a prayer to God. This is why complaining is not a prayer, even though it is a form of fellowship, because of the time spent. It doesn't produce desired results, but prayer does (**Numbers 11:1**).

Enhancer: Fasting

Finally, fasting is for a period of time. As such, what we forgo in fasting are simply things that are not necessarily sins but are capable of distracting us or making it harder to connect with God. Fasting means abstinence, and it is for an interval of time. It entails intentionally denying ourselves of some things to focus on God alone. The things we give up to focus on God are not necessarily sinful; they have the potential to impede our connection with God. The primary kind of fasting is abstinence from food. However, there are many other kinds of fasting. Sacrificial fasting entails removing anything that can interrupt or disrupt our fellowship time with God. We can also fast from social media, entertainment, and so on. Regardless of the kind of fast we are observing, a few things must be involved for it to be beneficial. We can find these things in **Matthew 6:16-18 NLT**. Jesus said, "*When you fast, don't make it obvious, as the hypocrites do, for they try to look miserable and disheveled so people will admire them for their fasting. I tell you the truth, that is the only reward they will ever get. But when you fast, comb your hair and wash your face. Then no one will notice that you are fasting except your Father, who knows what you do in private. And your Father, who sees everything, will reward you.*" We must understand that the purpose of fasting is so we can fellowship with God. Therefore, our fasting is only beneficial when it is between God and us.

Fasting is a fellowship enhancer. It enables us to eliminate hindrances and distractions when engaging in fellowship. This enhancer cannot generate results when engaged alone. It must be coupled with any or all of the fellowship methods discussed previously to create results or achieve goals. There are other benefits to fasting. From a physical perspective, fasting can benefit the human body or physical health. From a spiritual perspective, fasting enables Spirit-filled children of God to develop their spiritual muscles. In **Isaiah 58:8-9**, we see that when fasting is done correctly, we have access to God's treasure. Hence, the right kind of fasting opens the door to treasures. However, when fasting is not coupled with prayer, worship, and the Word, it becomes voluntary starvation or deprivation.

Fellowship with Human

There is a saying that "no man is an island." This is true because human connections and relationships are the bedrock of a healthy lifestyle. Conversely, lack of fellowship and human connection contributes to the high rate of depression and suicide. Have you ever wondered why you are born into a family? In an ideal state, each person has a father, mother, and other family members. But, anyone with any achievement had some human support as an enabler.

God created us to be interdependent. This was why He said in **Genesis 2:18 NLT**, "*It is not good for the man to be alone. I will make a helper who is just right for him.*" Let's think this through, in **Genesis 1:31**, after the creation of man, God called man very good. This means that the statement in **Genesis 2:18** shows that making humans interdependent was God's intention all along. It is, therefore, an illusion to think that we can be fully independent.

Human connection is inevitable. Even Jesus could not achieve His mandate without human fellowship. It took human fellowship to bring about the era of the Holy Spirit (**Acts 2:1**). As mentioned earlier, whatever we spend time doing with another human is fellowship. Therefore, it is essential to understand that any fellowship will either add to us or subtract from us; it never leaves us the same.

To get the best out of our human interactions, the Bible advises us in **Hebrews 10:25 NLT** to "*not neglect our meeting together, as some people do, but encourage one another,* *especially now that the day of his return is drawing near."* This is because "birds of a feather flock together." When we fellowship with the right people, we grow together, succeed together, and achieve together. If you wish to grow in any area of life, fellowship with the right person (in that area) who can add value to your life.

As children of God, the Holy Spirit is not an option we choose when it's convenient, He is a necessity. You may ask why the Holy Spirit is necessary here. One of the necessities of fellowship is trust. We know from **Jeremiah 17:9 NLT** that "*The human heart is the most deceitful of all things, and desperately wicked. Who really knows how bad it is?*". However, the Holy *Spirit searches out everything and shows us God's deep secrets* (**1 Corinthians 2:10 NLT**). Therefore, we need the Holy Spirit to lead us to obtain the treasure of human fellowship without getting burned.

OBEDIENCE

Obedience is critical to experiencing any growth in God. Therefore, there is no replacement or substitute for obedience.

First, as children of God, we are commanded to be like God (**1 Peter 1:16**). If this is our goal, then we must know that the one we listen to is the one we become. Therefore, to be like God, we must listen to Him. In this case, to listen to God is to obey Him.

Secondly, though God is not a slavemaster (because He does not force us to do anything), **Romans 8:14 NLT** says all who the Spirit of God leads are children of God. To be led means to be willingly obedient. We can see that obedience qualifies us as children of God. But why? We must understand that disobedience is a sign of distrust, a lack of faith.

When we disobey God, He cannot trust us; as such, He will not release His secrets to us (**James 1:6-8**). As we have learnt, God only shares His secrets with those He trusts. If we are to grow in God, then we need the mysteries of God. Obedience shows God that He can trust us and give us more secrets (**Deuteronomy 29:29**).

"God's precept must be upon precept, precept upon precept, Line upon line, line upon line, Here a little, there a little." (**Isaiah 28:10 NKJV, emphasis added**) We cannot handle every assignment God wants us to do or all the information He wants to share with us at once. A step-by-step process is needed; that is, precept upon precept. For example, there are different stages of growth in the physical, and each stage has its unique requirement and expectation. This is the same in the spiritual. In the spiritual, obedience qualifies us and grants us access to more of God and more from God. Our spiritual growth is hinged on our obedience to God. We can only move to the next stage of development when we have obeyed God's instructions at our current stage. John Bevere said, "spiritual maturity is tied to obedience and not time." This is why we see immature Christians who have been in God for a long time. Perhaps, obedience is the missing key in their case.

The good news is that we serve a God who knows the measure we can handle, so He starts with us at our current level of maturity. It is essential to know that everything pertaining to God starts small. If anything starts big, I can assure you it is not of God. All the giants of scriptures began small. From Moses to Joseph and King David, and even Jesus, the Messiah, there was a time of small beginning. Therefore, Do not despise these small beginnings, for the LORD rejoices to see the work begin (**Zachariah 4:10a**).

Even though things may start small, they can be enormous. Hence, if anything starts big without any trace of a small beginning, it is demonic.

Lastly, let us dive into Jesus' response to a very critical question in **Matthew 22:36-40 NLT,**

"Teacher, which is the most important commandment in the law of Moses?" Jesus replied, "'You must love the Lord your God with all your heart, all your soul, and all your mind.' This is the first and greatest commandment. A second is equally important: 'Love your neighbor as yourself.' The entire law and all the demands of the prophets are based on these two commandments."

The scripture above shows that the law of love is the most important according to our savior, Jesus. The first component of love in accordance with Jesus' response was, *"we must love the Lord our God with all our heart, soul and mind."* A logical question here becomes, how do we do this? The answer to this question is in **John 14:15 NLT**; Jesus said, *"if you love me, obey my commandments."* When we substitute this answer into the first scripture, it reads, *"we must OBEY OUR LORD'S COMMAND with all our heart, soul and mind."* In accordance with our previous studies, we see that our obedience is an act of love, and love is an act of worship. As such, obedience can be seen as a spiritual exercise that enhances spiritual growth. Conversely, disobedience is interpreted as a lack of love for God; it stunts our spiritual growth.

KINGDOM GREATNESS

The moment we receive Jesus, we are a new creation (**2 Corinthians 5:17**). Therefore, we do not function or live like carnal men. We are human but don't wage war as humans do (**2 Corinthians 10:3 NLT**). We exist in the kingdom of God in both the physical and spiritual (**Colossians 1:13**). Many believe that the Kingdom of God is only in the afterlife; this is partly true because there is another side to the coin. Let's examine an incident in **Luke 17:20-21 NLT**.

One day the Pharisees asked Jesus, "When will the Kingdom of God come?" Jesus replied, "The Kingdom of God can't be detected by visible signs. You won't be able to say, 'Here it is!' or 'It's over there!' For the Kingdom of God is already among you.

In this scripture above, Jesus gave us the perspective of the other side of the coin. How is the kingdom of God already among us? In the Amplified version of the scripture, emphasis was added: *For the kingdom of God is among you [because of My presence].* This implies that the presence of Jesus was the Kingdom of God on earth at the time. The presence of Jesus brought heaven to earth. We can argue that when Jesus ascended to heaven, He took the kingdom of God with Him. This is true; however, before Jesus left the earth, He promised us a replacement of His physical presence in the person of the Holy Spirit (**John 14:16-17**). In His promise, He assured us that the Holy Spirit would never leave us. Consequently, the presence of the Holy Spirit, who is also God, is a re-enactment of the kingdom of God among us. The Spirit of God gives us a taste of the kingdom of God here on earth, just as Jesus did (**Romans 8:23**). His presence even takes it further because He is within us and with us at all times (**John 14:17**). Therefore, we are living in heaven on earth, because of the salvation work of Jesus and the presence of the Holy Spirit unleashed in us and on the earth.

God's plan is for everyone to be on top and never beneath. The scripture in **Deuteronomy 28:13 NLT** took me a while to understand. The Bible says, *"if you carefully obey them, the LORD will make you the head and not the tail, and you will always be on top and never at the bottom."* Looking at this scripture, I had questions. I understood that all the promises of God are for His children. And, of course, obedience was imperative to enjoy the blessings (**Isaiah 1:19**). However, does this mean that every child of God is destined for the top? If that is the case, who will be at the bottom? Also, if everyone is saved, who will be at the bottom? These were some of my questions until understanding came from God. Everything of God has the potential to be big, and so does every child of God. As per **Psalm 82:6**, a child of God is a god. Therefore, every child of God has the potential to be great.

When I presented my questions to the Lord, He explained the following. He said if humans can build a system that allows many airplanes to fly simultaneously, and sometimes at the same altitude with minimal risk for collision, then it is possible for every single child of God to be at the top simultaneously. This was an eye-opener that made me understand that jealousy was simply unnecessary among the children of God. We must realize that every airplane has the potential to fly high; however, their takeoff times may be different. For instance, when airplane A is at cruising altitude, airplane B may still be taxing down the runway. This is why patience is a virtue and the fruit of the Holy Spirit.

As children of God, we can all be at the top simultaneously without affecting or destroying each other. From **Deuteronomy 28:13**, we see that obedience is needed to attain this height. In the scripture below, Jesus zoomed in on another critical element for being the greatest in the kingdom of God. That is, the kingdom here on earth and in the afterlife.

After they arrived at Capernaum and settled in a house, Jesus asked his disciples, "What were you discussing out on the road?" But they didn't answer, because they had been arguing about which of them was the greatest. He sat down, called the twelve disciples over to him, and said, "Whoever wants to be first must take last place and be the servant of everyone else." Then he put a little child among them. Taking the child in his arms, he said to them, "Anyone who welcomes a little child like this on my behalf welcomes me, and anyone who welcomes me welcomes not only me but also my Father who sent me." (**Mark 9:33-37 NLT**)

This scripture also buttresses the point that God wants us all to be above. Jesus gave the secret for getting to the top to all His disciples; He did not restrict it to His inner circle (Peter, James and John). God also reinforced this intention for all His children to be at the top in the books of Matthew, Mark and Luke.

Looking at that scripture again, Jesus pointed out two fundamental principles that must be upheld to be the greatest—humility and honor. Humility and honor are equally important. Growth in God is directly proportional to humility and honor. As you engage both principles, your growth in God is enhanced. We have been redeemed into the kingdom of God through Jesus (**Colossians 1:13-14**). Growth in God's spiritual world is simply growth in the kingdom of God. The higher we grow, the more of the kingdom treasures we enjoy.

Humility

Jesus said *whoever wants to be first must take last place and be the servant of everyone else.* This is the true meaning of humility from God's point of view. I understand that this sounds insane and degrading. But we must first understand that Jesus was not talking to everybody here. He was addressing His disciples. Even today, this definition of humility is not for everybody. It is for those who are indeed under God's leadership through Jesus. Hence, the concept of humility is meant only for the disciples of Jesus. Those who are already translated into the kingdom of God through Jesus (**Colossians 1:13**) and sealed by the power of the Holy Spirit (**Ephesians 1:13**).

Humility is the way of life in the kingdom of God, to which we belong. To ascend, we must first descend (**Ephesians 4:9**). In the words of my father in the Lord, "the way up in this kingdom is down." Anyone great in this kingdom was once down. As we have established earlier, everything that pertains to God starts small. It was not until Jesus humbled Himself that He was exalted and given a name above all (**Philippians 2:8-9**). Therefore, humility is not low self-esteem. The definition of humility stems from **Revelations 5:10**, where it was revealed that we had been redeemed as Kings and Priests on this earth. We are kings because of our relationship with God; we are disciples of Jesus and Children of the Most High. As such, we are destined for the top (**Deuteronomy 28:13**). We are priests to serve others (**Galatians 5:13**). As such, it is our job to preach the gospel to all (**Mark 16:15**) and love our neighbors as we love ourselves (**Mark 12:31**). Therefore, humility is the act of knowing ourselves first as disciples of Jesus; only then can we truly humble ourselves and serve others.

Service without initial knowledge of our identity is work birthed out of low self-esteem. It is impossible to affirm our humility until we know who we are. In the same manner, identity without service is pride. Our service or identity alone does not make us humble. The true definition of humility is when service and identity are combined in the correct quantity and coupled with love. Anything short of walking in your kingship identity and priestly role indicates the presence of pride or low self-esteem.

As per my spiritual father, "we come to humility when we know that God uses others as well as He uses us." No man is an island. You are a product of your relationships, and you become who you give your ears. Therefore, as kings, we must understand that there are other kings with grace and more extraordinary grace. *God opposes the proud but gives grace to the humble (*James 4:6). As we identify different kinds of grace and humble ourselves in service, grace is added to us. Therefore, we must know ourselves and acknowledge the grace of God over other kings. It is humility that will allow the iron to sharpen iron (**Proverbs 27:17**); it takes humility to get to the top and stay at the top. This is a perfect segue into the second thing Jesus mentioned.

Honor

Jesus said, *"anyone who welcomes a little child like this on my behalf welcomes me, and anyone who welcomes me welcomes not only me but also my Father who sent me."* In this scripture, Jesus was talking about honor. He said that regardless of age when we honor anyone because of the grace of God on them, we are on our way to the top. Jesus was teaching that the person we welcome, we receive. *"If you receive a prophet as one who speaks for God, you will be given the same reward as a prophet. And if you receive righteous people because of their righteousness, you will be given a reward like theirs"* (**Matthew 10:41 NLT**). Honor opens the door for us to receive the same reward as the person we give. To put this into perspective, honor is the fastest route to the top. What an individual might have to obtain through fasting can be obtained through honor. Therefore, when we see our giant brothers and sisters in the faith, it is not petty to honor them; it is instead a highway to the top. The presence of grace may not be obvious in their lives, but through discernment, patterns, and results being generated, it is evident. Once the grace is identified, one way to gain access to the grace is through honor. For instance, we can gain access to the grace to live long when we honor our father and mother because they are the agents of life (**Ephesians 6:2-3**). It is imperative to know that God is the source of life, but He has delegated this life by giving grace to our parents. Similarly, suppose you want to be at the top in any specific area of life. In that case, you must let God lead you to someone carrying the grace in that area of life so that you can honor them as God gives you the opportunity.

Honor is simply welcoming and receiving another disciple-grace carrier. It is respecting the grace of God on another disciple—regardless of age, status, or social class. We should respect, receive, and welcome any disciple of Jesus because of God's grace. My father in the Lord always says, "when you get to a place for the first time, it is wise to locate the human head of the place and honor them."

The Recipe

To be humble, we must know who we are, recognize others with grace and put their needs ahead of ours. Recognizing others and putting their needs ahead of ours is the true definition of Honor. We can see that we cannot be humble without honor and vice versa.

Humility and honor cause us to grow because it gives God an opening to bestow on us the grace that we are honoring (**Matthew 10:41**).

God's principles are practical and can be applied to all aspects of life. The principle of humility and honor can be used in various settings. For example, suppose an individual wants to yield an increase in a country. In that case, they must first know their place in that country and honor the authorities of that country. Unfortunately, many people cannot succeed in a country because they have no respect for its authorities. Some are temporary residents purporting to be citizens; as such, their life is a mess. While some others are citizens with flagrant disregard for the authorities of the land—the rule of law, leaders et al. The fact remains that these authorities are ordained by God (**Romans 13:1**). Unless we follow the process, the blessings of that land will elude us.

In the same way, a child must distinguish their place from that of their parents within a family and honor their parents accordingly. As we have learnt, parents have delegated authority from God. Unless we honor them, we are not entitled to the blessings that flow from them (**Ephesians 6:2-3**). Regardless of their spiritual status, God has given the parents the grace for life; hence, they gave birth to us—biological life. Therefore, for life we have received from our parents to be sustained and prolonged, we must honor them (**Ephesians 6:2-3**).

Wherever we find ourselves, humility and honor are imperative if we aim to be above and not beneath. We must understand that it is God who rewards us. If the intentions behind our actions are not pure, they will not yield the desired results. Genuine humility and honor flow from the heart. The outward expression of what we do is only a reflection of the substance within our heart (**Proverbs 23:7**). There are many things to be said here, but I pray that the Spirit of God will give you more light in Jesus' name. Amen!

The Mystery of Consistency

Now that we have outlined different things, it is important we understand what makes everything run smoothly. In the physical, we see the benefits from exercise when we engage consistently. The moment we stop exercising, the benefits that have been accrued gradually dissipates, and we eventually revert back to the pre-exercise state. The same holds true in the spiritual.

A while back, the Lord showed me something that opened my eyes to the mystery we are about to discuss here. The Holy Spirit drew my attention to something very interesting about the gathering of saints. Every time the saints gather, God is always there to do all kinds of great things. **Matthew 18:20** NLT confirms this, *"for where two or three gathers together as my followers, I am there among them."* But the Lord explained to me that He will always move in the gathering of the saints because it is an appointment with God. God is never late and He will always show up to an appointment, as long as He was consulted and/or informed about the gathering. When we consistently show up, God will always reveal Himself.

In a God-ordained ministry, gatherings are based on God's sanction. In so doing, God is aware of their coming. For example, the regular services at my home church, including the time for each service, were dictated by God at the inception of the church. Hence, regardless of the number of congregants, God will be present at the scheduled time. On no account do we change the service day or service time, even if it coincides with a statutory holiday; we strictly comply with God's ordination.

In the same way, it is wisdom to set a personal appointment with God to engage in spiritual exercises. I highly recommend that we fellowship with God daily at an appointed time. As for fasting, we must have a consistent time as well. Let heaven know the time you have chosen to meet and fellowship with the Lord. Furthermore, there are occasions when God will determine the time He wants you to fellowship with Him. Whatever the case maybe, ensure you remain diligent with the appointment no matter the circumstance.

It is also important to note that even though consistency is crucial, it does not negate the fact that we are God's children. As such, God can reorder the structure of our quiet time with Him as He pleases. For example, the Lord might prompt us to fast every day in a particular week, even though we had originally set out to do so once that week. When this happens, there is no need to fret, just submit and follow the leading of His Spirit.

From scriptures, we see that those that have quality relationships with God are those that consistently show up for their appointment with God. For example, David, a man after God's heart (**1 Samuel 13:14**), said *"I will praise you seven times a day because all your regulations are just"* (**Psalm 119:164 NLT**). Daniel, a man with an excellent Spirit (**Daniel 5:12**), *prayed three times a day, just as he had always done, giving thanks to his God* (**Daniel 6:10 NLT**). This is the only way we can consistently grow in God. What we do constantly is what yields good results.

Lastly, we must understand that any human being operating without the help of the Holy Spirit will get carried away by the issues of life. Therefore, when we set a time to fellowship with God, we must ask God for grace, *because It is not by force nor by strength, but by my Spirit, says the LORD of Heaven's Armies* (**Zachariah 4:6b NLT**). We must make out time for the things that are most important.

Chapter 5

Conclusion

The content of this book is not the totality of spiritual development. It is only the beginning of a fantastic walk with God. The steps outlined in this book will create a solid foundation for the Spirit of God to build on. This book aims to facilitate the understanding that walking closely with God and growing in God is simple and attainable. It may seem tedious or impossible, but it is not. I believe that it is not God when anything becomes complicated, challenging or wearisome. God is not in the business of making things difficult or impossible for us. The ease of life comes from God (**James 1:17**). However, we must be willing to pay the price because nothing of value comes easy.

Here are the simple foundational steps to a close relationship with God.

- Accept Jesus as your Lord and Savior as outlined in **Romans 10:9**. If you wish to understand why this is necessary, please read the book I authored, "The

Person You Should Know." Otherwise, you can say this simple prayer:

Dear heavenly Father,
I thank You for sending Your son Jesus to die on the cross for my sins. I know I am a sinner in need of a savior. I confess my sin and ask You for forgiveness. I believe that Jesus died for my sins, and You raised Him to claim my victory. I confess and accept Jesus as my personal Lord and Savior and invite Him into my heart. With your help, I will trust and obey You forever. So, help me, God, in Jesus' name. Amen.

If you said the prayer above, congratulations! Welcome to the kingdom of God. Please get in touch with me using the information in the section, Contact the Author. I will be happy to provide you with resources to help you grow in God.

o Receive the Baptism of the Holy Spirit. As we have learnt from this book, as children of God, the Holy Spirit is not an option but a necessity. The Bible made us understand that we are sealed in God with the Holy Spirit (**Ephesian 4:30**). Also, we are only a child of God if we are led by the Holy Spirit (**Romans 8:14**). Therefore, if we do not have the Holy Spirit, we are not sealed, and we can lose our salvation. Until we receive the Holy Spirit, we will not have access to many things in God. If you require more insight into the Person of the Holy Spirit, please read the book I authored, "The Most Important Person of Our Time."

You can receive the Holy Spirit by asking God (**Luke 11:13**). Though I strongly encourage you to consult a person with a proven track record of their walk with the Holy Spirit to help you in this process.

- Finally, take the steps as outlined in this book by faith. As you do so, you will start getting closer and closer to God. The closer you get, the more you recognize His voice (**John 10:27**). As such, He will begin to lead, guide, instruct, and help you beyond the content of this book.

I pray that as you embark on this growth journey in God, may He who has faithfully *begun the good work within you continue his work until it is finally finished on the day Christ Jesus returns* (**Philippians 1:6 NLT**). Amen! God bless you.

New Believer's Prayer

Dear Heavenly Father,
I thank You for sending Your son Jesus to die on the cross for my sins. I know I am a sinner in need of a savior. I confess my sin and ask You for forgiveness. I believe that Jesus died for my sins, and You raised Him to claim my victory. I confess and accept Jesus as my personal Lord and Savior and invite Him into my heart. With your help, I will trust and obey You forever. So, help me, God, in Jesus' name. Amen

Contact the Author

I am sure this book has blessed you, and it will be my joy to hear from you. You can reach me at info@eagboola.com. For more information about me, please visit my website at www.eagboola.com.

God bless you.

About the Book

One of the illusions today is that the things of God are complex, tedious, or complicated. From our thinking, this might seem justified because humans cannot fathom God. However, we see from **2 Corinthians 11:3 NKJV** that this is far from the truth. According to scripture, God, who made us (**Genesis 1:27**), wants us to be close to Him. When Adam fell, God went to great lengths to restore humanity to Himself. This cost Him Jesus, who died for us (**John 3:16**).

If God can do all this to reach us, why will He make it difficult to get closer to Him? In **James 4:8**, the Bible affirms that if we come close to God, He will come close to us. This means that if we come close to Him as He has outlined in His Word, that is, through Jesus, He will come closer and dwell with us (**Revelations 3:20**). In fact, anytime we encounter anything that seems complicated, tedious, or challenging, there is a chance that the hand of God is not in it. In these cases, we should invite God in. Advancing to a phase of significant growth in God from salvation is a simple journey with the help of the Holy Spirit. The gift of the Holy Spirit, called the word of wisdom, is God's attempt to simplify complicated things. From the account of the Bible, every time humans expressed that the things of God were hard, God went above and beyond to make it very easy

(Judges 6-8). For example, to become a child of God only requires a simple prayer. In the same way, to grow in God only requires simple steps. God is not out to get us so He can judge us; He is out to get us to have a closer relationship with Him.

With the help of the Holy Spirit, this book provides light and insight from God. It contains practical foundational steps to a less complicated growth in God. Relax and enjoy as the Spirit of God takes you through a simple growth journey, as outlined in this book.

Other Books by the Author

1. The Person You Should Know
2. The Most Important Act
3. The Most Important Person of Our Time
4. The Blueprint of Relationships
5. Own Your Destiny

Ebenezer Agboola is a teacher in the body of Christ by calling. The core of his call is to bring the light of understanding into the darkness of deception by teaching the word of God. He believes that ignorance is bondage and that understanding is freedom with its source from the Holy Spirit (2 Corinthians 3:17). Hence, his passion is seeing people seek understanding and apply it correctly (wisdom). The nature of his call makes him relevant not just to Christians but to everyone. He is a *Christian Apologist* whose passion is to bring the reality and practicality of God to reality.

He has authored books like The Person You Should Know, The Most Important Person of Our Time and various others to enhance growth in God. He is also the founding teaching minister of a teaching ministry called "The Ministry of Light international" (MOLI). The ministry organizes conferences and teaching events led by the Holy Spirit, where Ebenezer serves as the host minister.

He is happily married to Tumininu, and they are blessed with a lovely daughter Deborah.

www.ingramcontent.com/pod-product-compliance
Lightning Source LLC
Chambersburg PA
CBHW030304100526
44590CB00012B/510